KERBER PHOTO

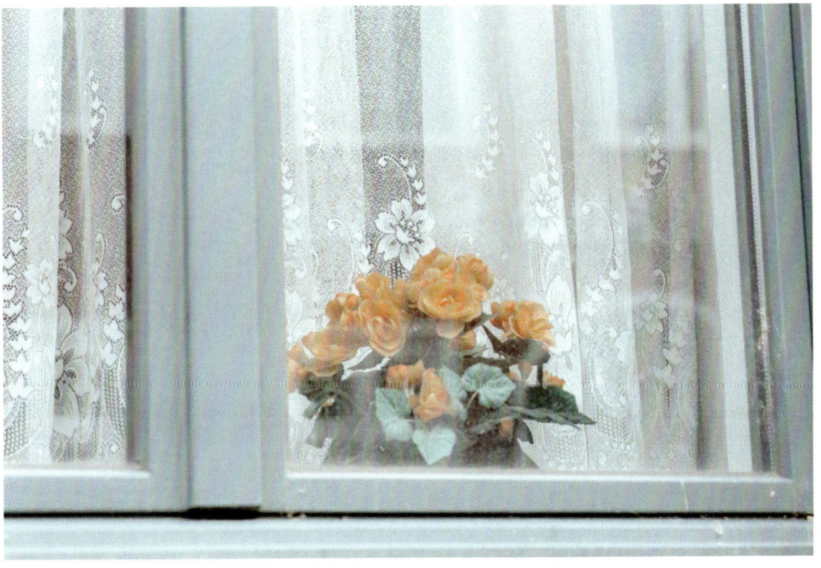

IRIS FRIEDRICH

GRAUMELIERT

pepper and salt

Vielleicht solltest Du doch mal über eine Veröffentlichung Deiner Stadtbilder nachdenken ...

Schönen Gruß aus Berlin

Michael

Oje, im Vermarkten bin ich gar nicht gut

Das Vermarkten übernimmt ja dann der Verlag ;-))

Der Zusammenhang in Deinen Stadtbildern liegt doch auf der Hand

Es ist eine Welt, die wir alle kennen, aber so klar nie gesehen haben. Die Qualität Deiner Bilder ist, dass sie neben dem ästhetischen Reiz einen leisen Humor haben und dass es mir beim Betrachten kalt über den Rücken läuft, weil ich denke: Verdammt, in dieser Welt bin ich aufgewachsen.

Das wäre dann jetzt schon das Vorwort ;-)

Dieser Wortwechsel mit dem Regisseur Michael Ammann legte den Grundstein für die Idee, an diesem Fotobuch zu arbeiten.

Dieses Projekt ist mir nachgelaufen. Oft entstehen meine Serien im Kopf, bevor sie umgesetzt werden. Das hier holte mich ein, während ich schon mittendrin steckte.

Einige meiner Bilder haben laufen gelernt. Die mit diesem Symbol A gekennzeichneten Fotografien haben eine „erweiterte Realität", diese „Augmented Reality"-Inhalte können Sie mit der App Artivive auf Ihr Smartphone zaubern und das Buch wird zur Bühne.

Maybe you should think about publishing your cityscapes ...

Greetings from Berlin

Michael

Oh no, self-marketing is not my key competence at all

The publishing house will take care of marketing then ;-))

The connection in your cityscapes is obvious

It is a world we all know but have never seen so clearly. The quality of your photographs is that, in addition to the aesthetic appeal, they have a quiet humor and it sends shivers down my spine when I look at them, because I think: Damn, this is the world I grew up in.

That would be already the preface now ;-)

This exchange of words with director Michael Ammann laid the ground for the idea to work on this photo book.

This project has grown unconsciously in me. Often, my series develop in my head before I realize them. This one caught up with me while I was already in the middle of it.

Some of my photographs have learned to walk. Photographs marked with the symbol A have an extended reality. You can conjure up this augmented reality content on your smartphone with the app Artivive and the photo book becomes a stage.

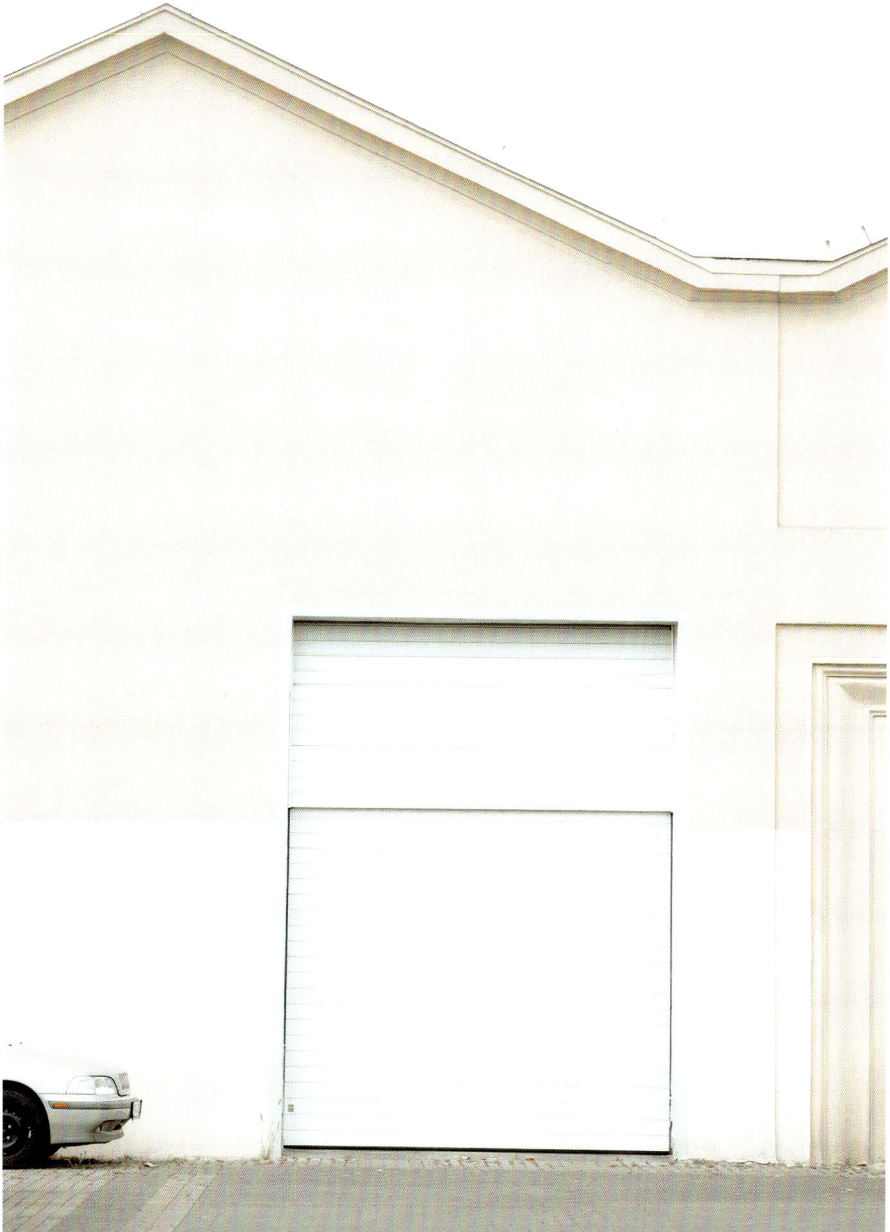

ARTIVIVE

Download on the App Store

GET IT ON Google Play

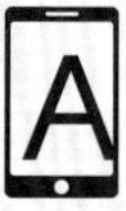

1. **Installieren** Sie die Artivive App

2. **Suchen** Sie mit diesem Symbol markierte Bilder

3. **Richten** Sie Ihr Smartphone je nach Symbol im Hoch- oder Querformat auf das Bild

1. **Install** the Artivive app

2. **Find** images marked with the Artivive icon

3. **View** the image through your smartphone. Depending on the icon, point your smartphone in portrait or landscape mode at the image

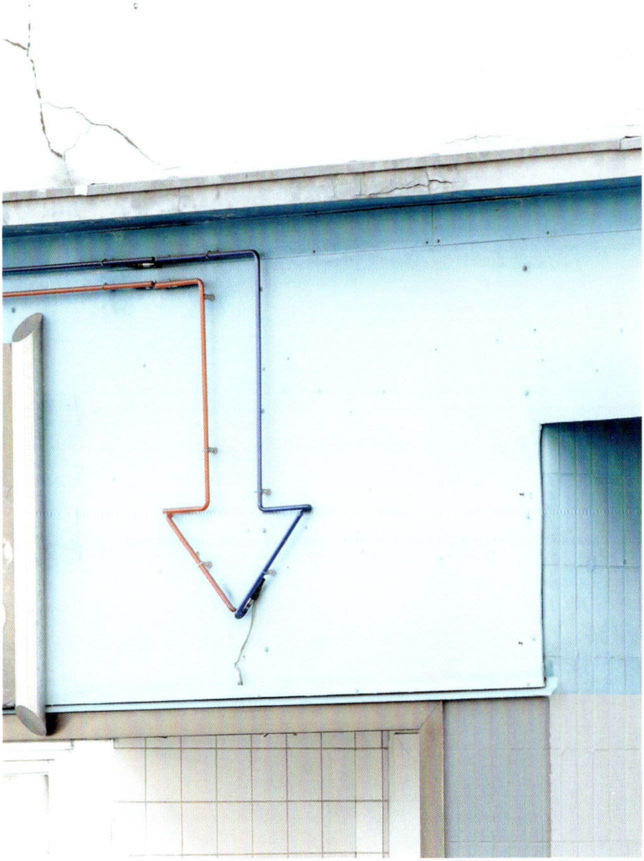

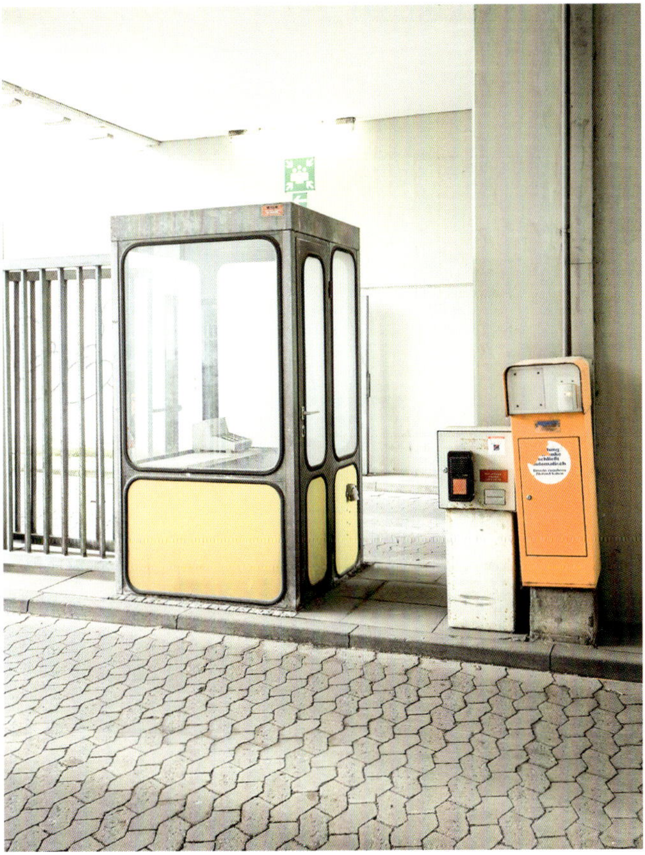

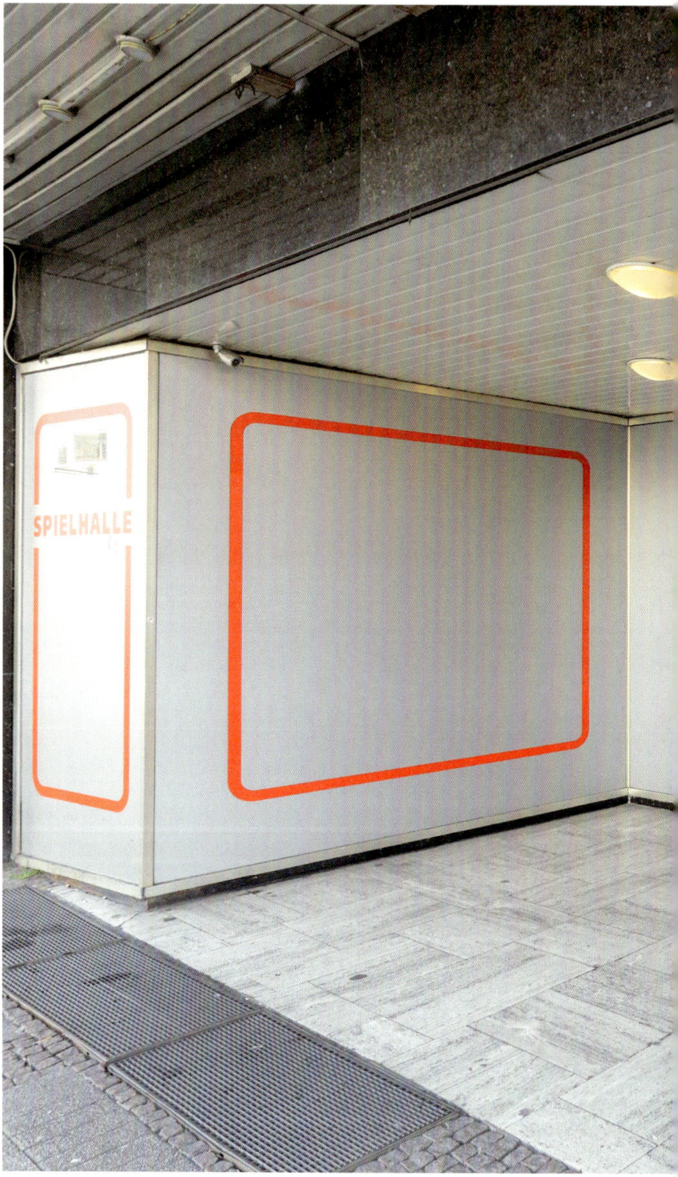
SPIELHALLE

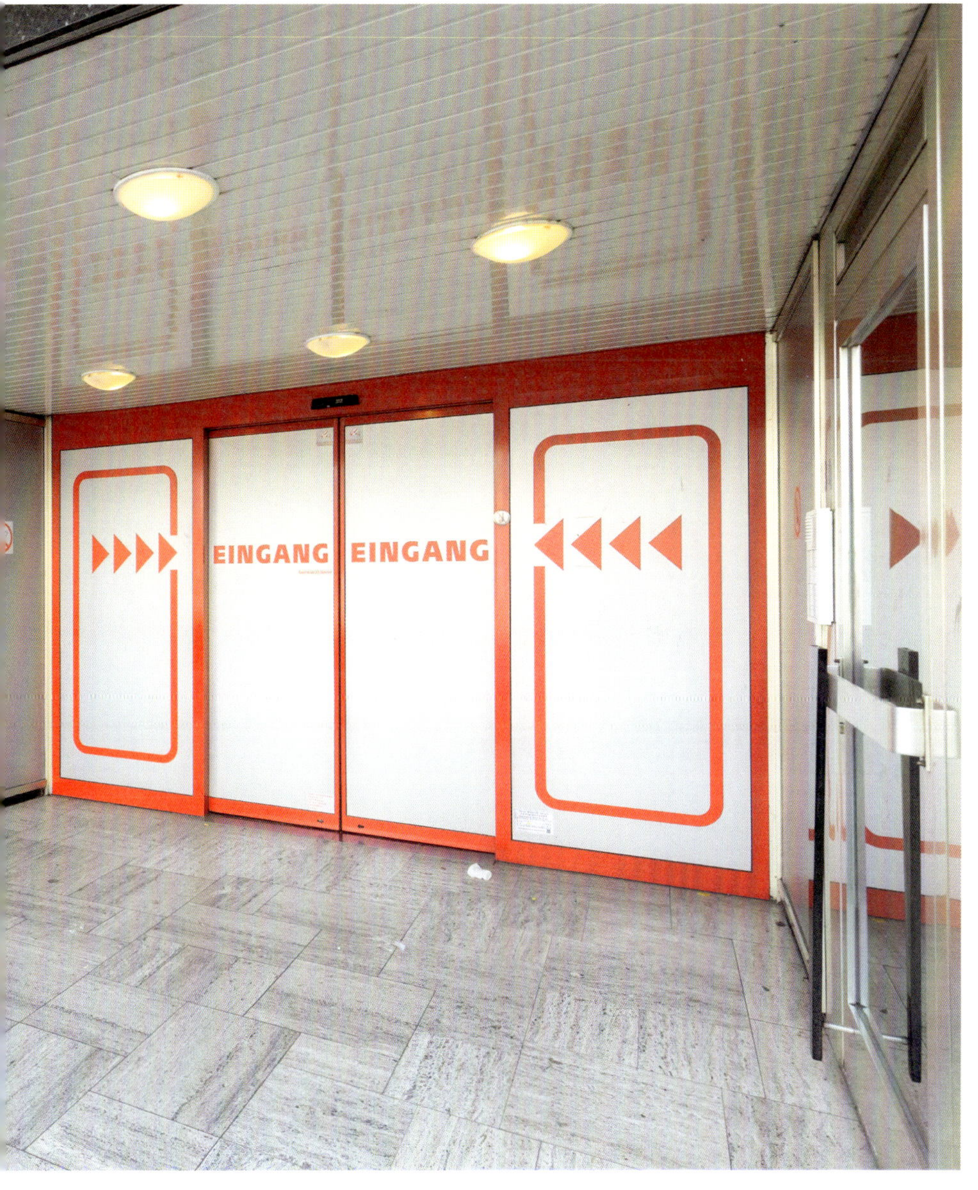
EINGANG
EINGANG

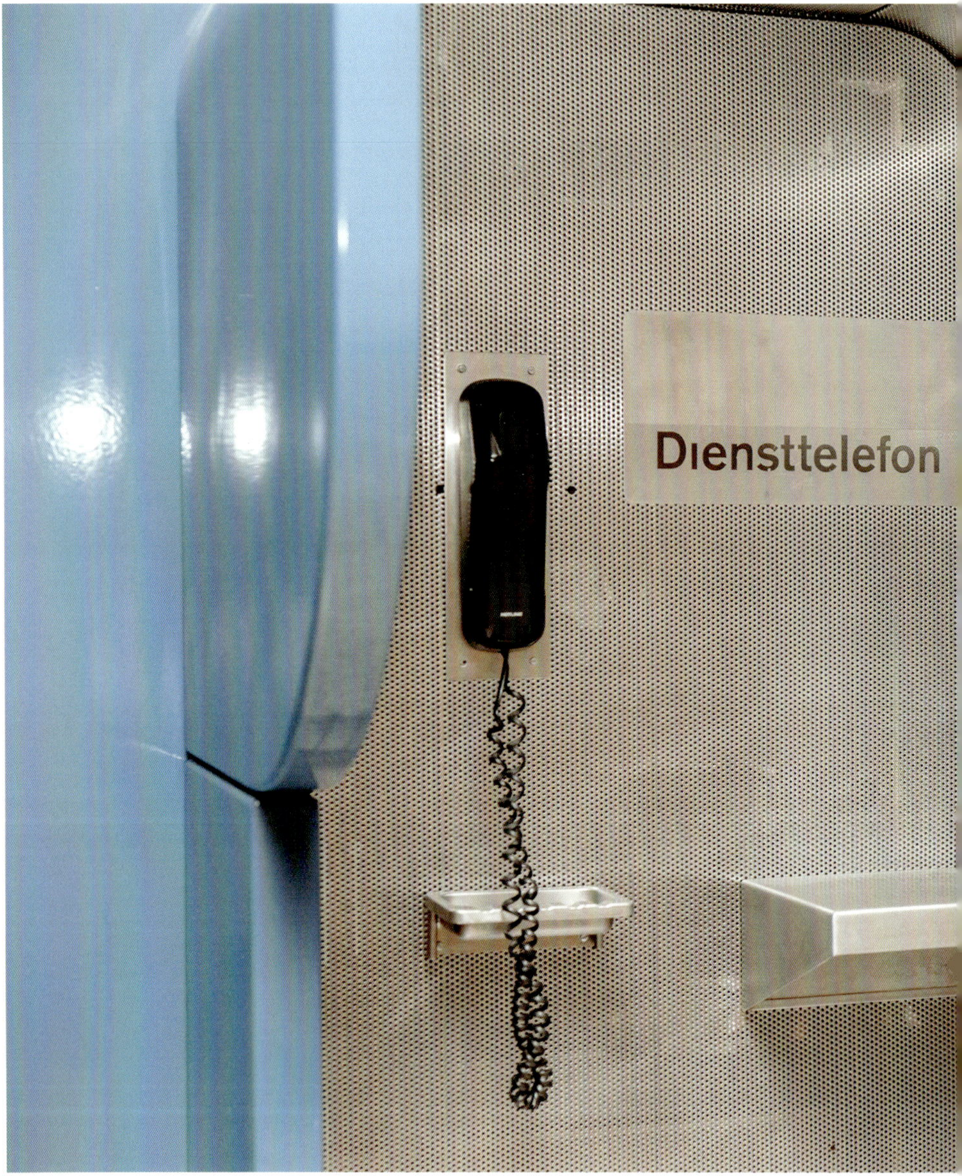
Diensttelefon

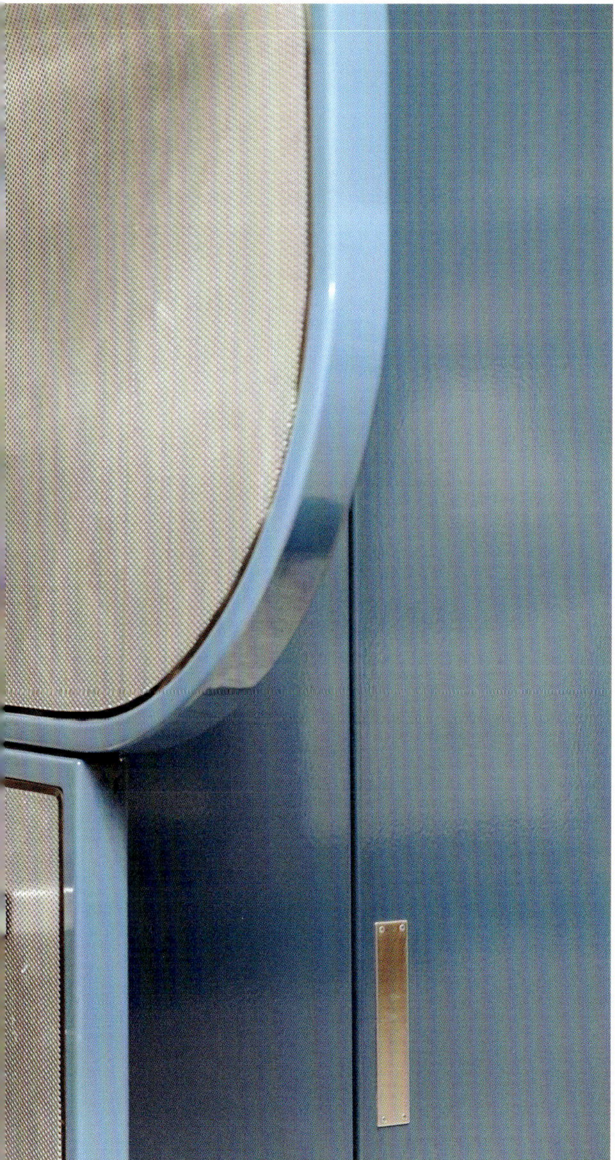

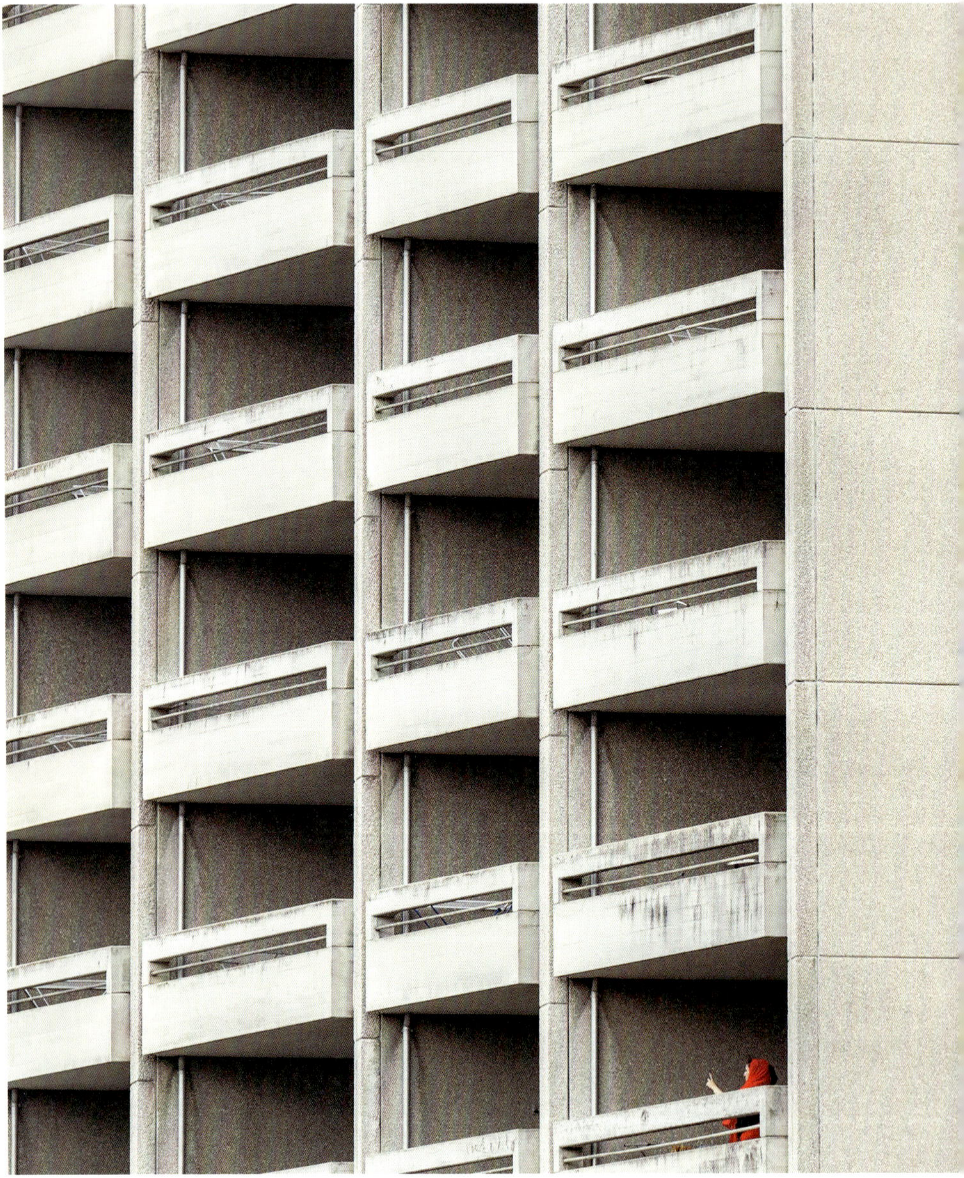

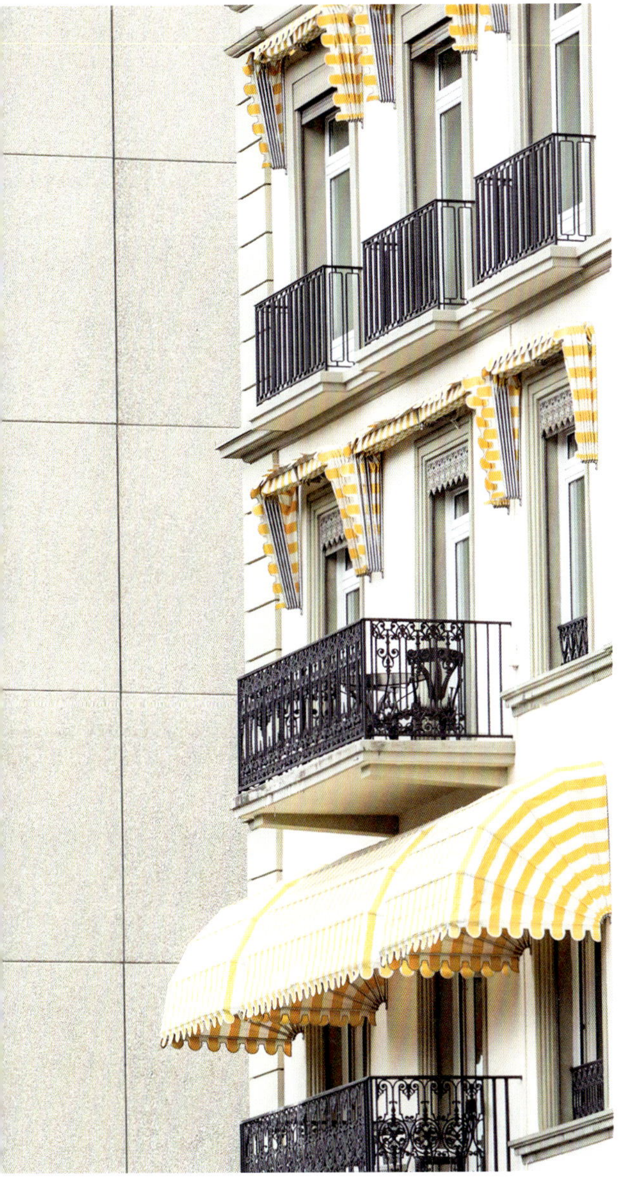

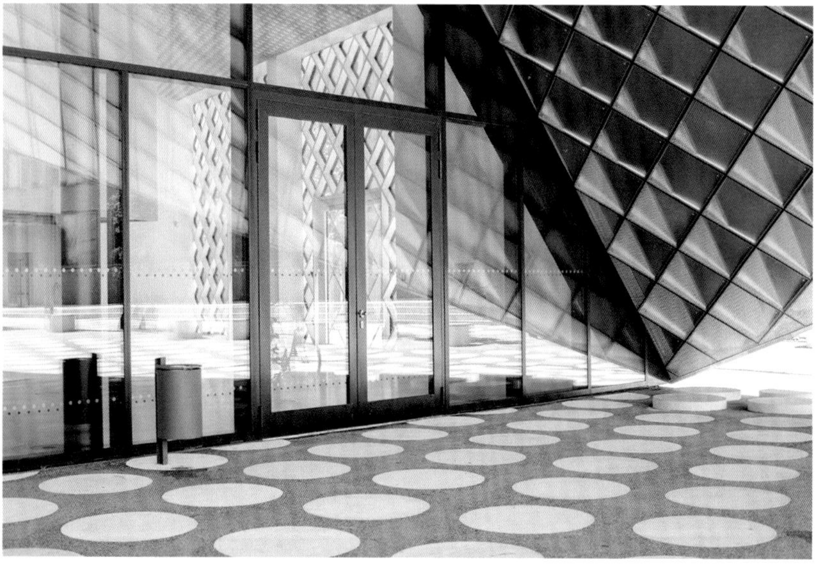

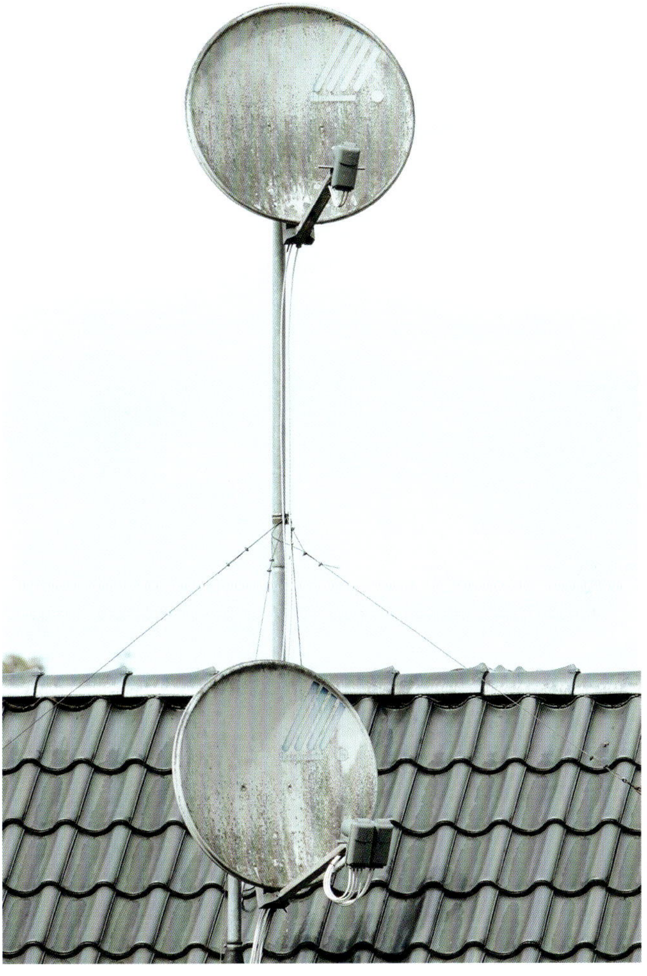

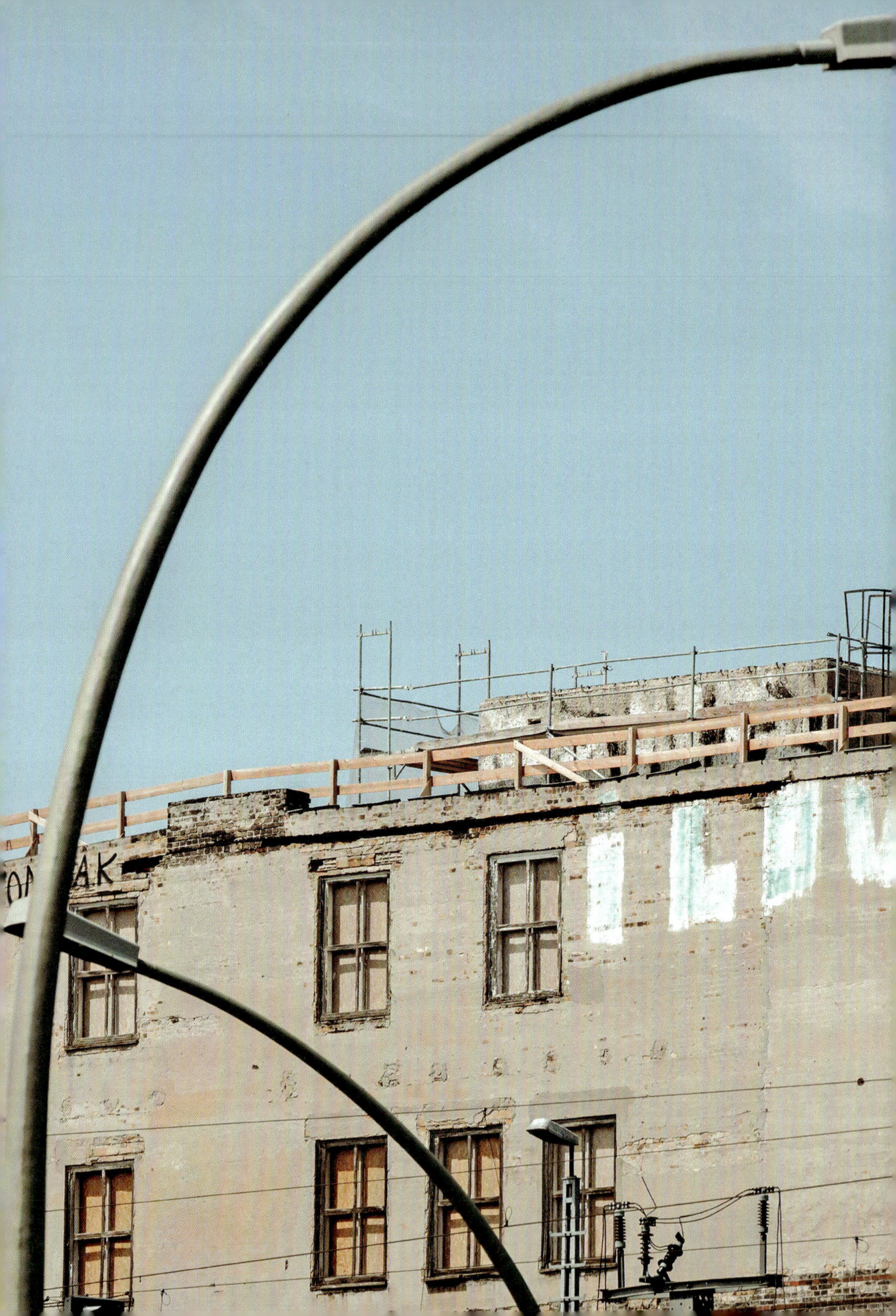

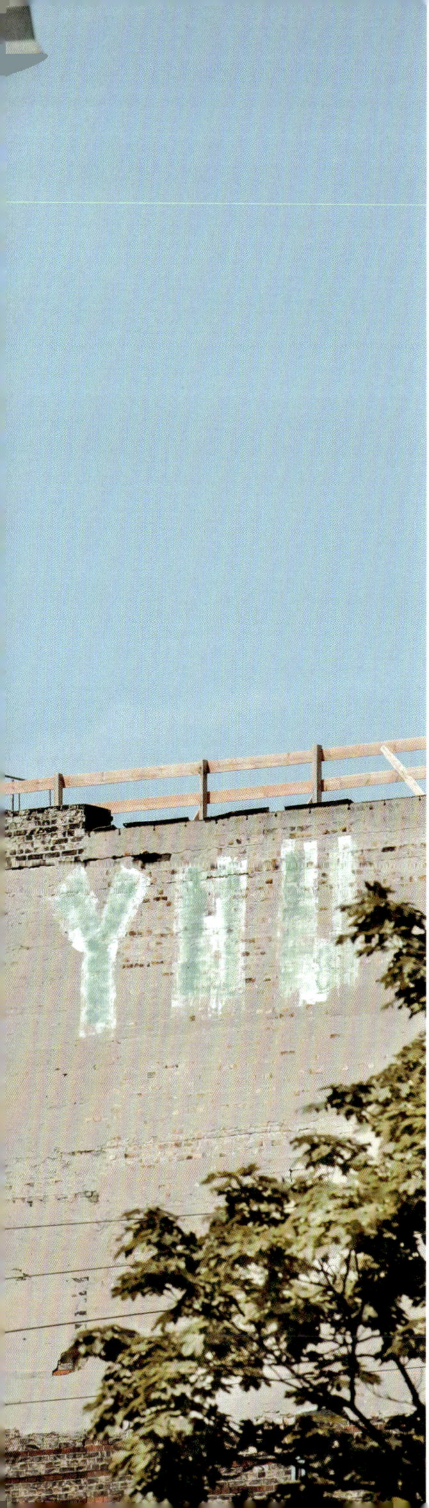

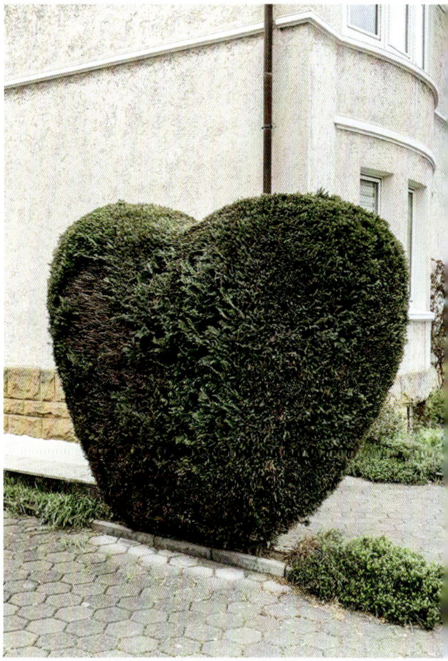

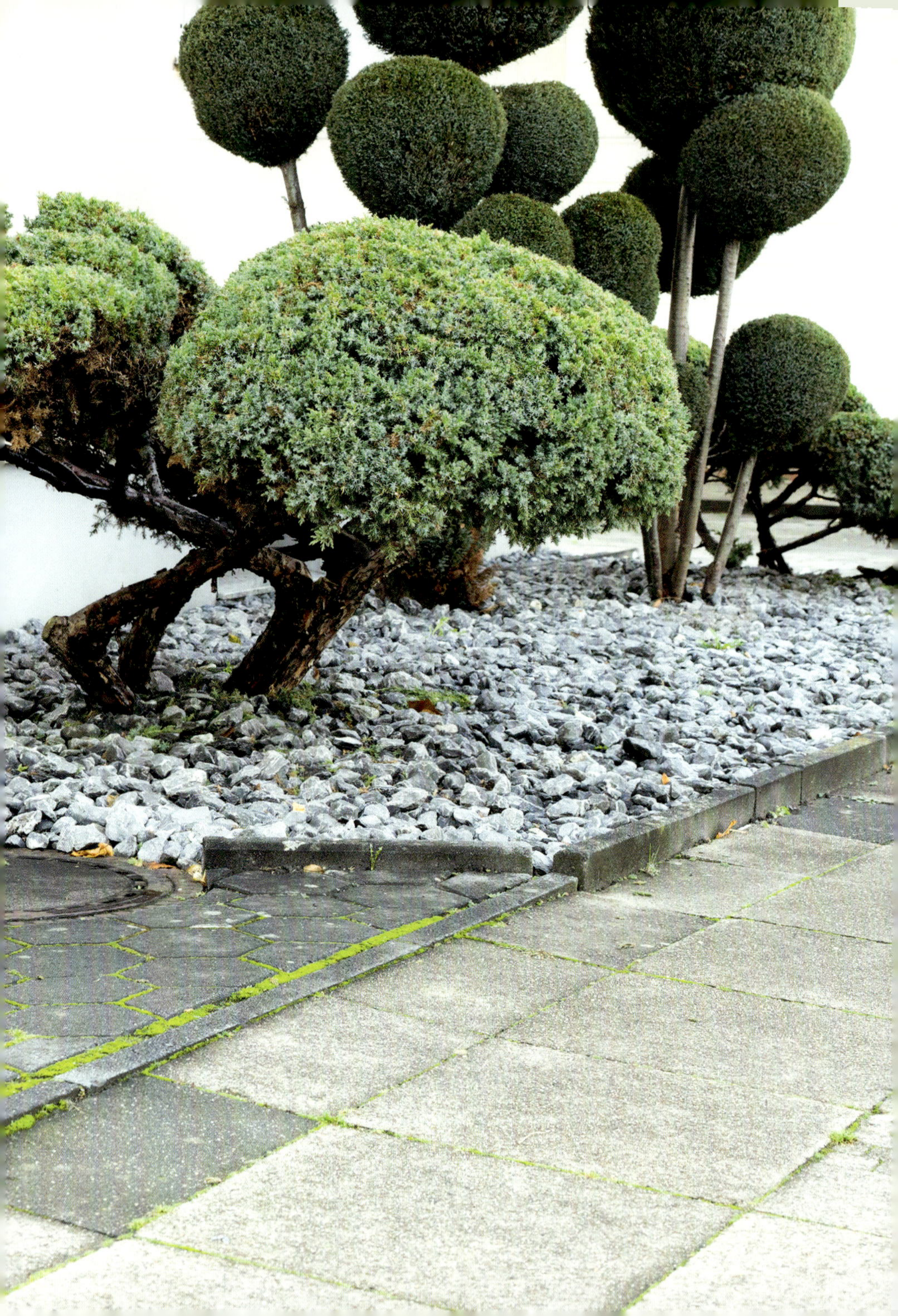

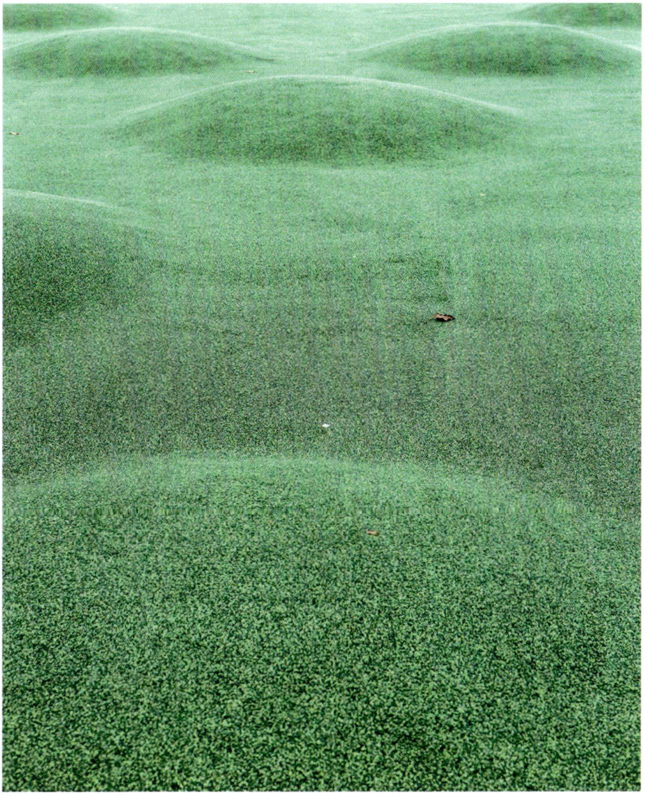

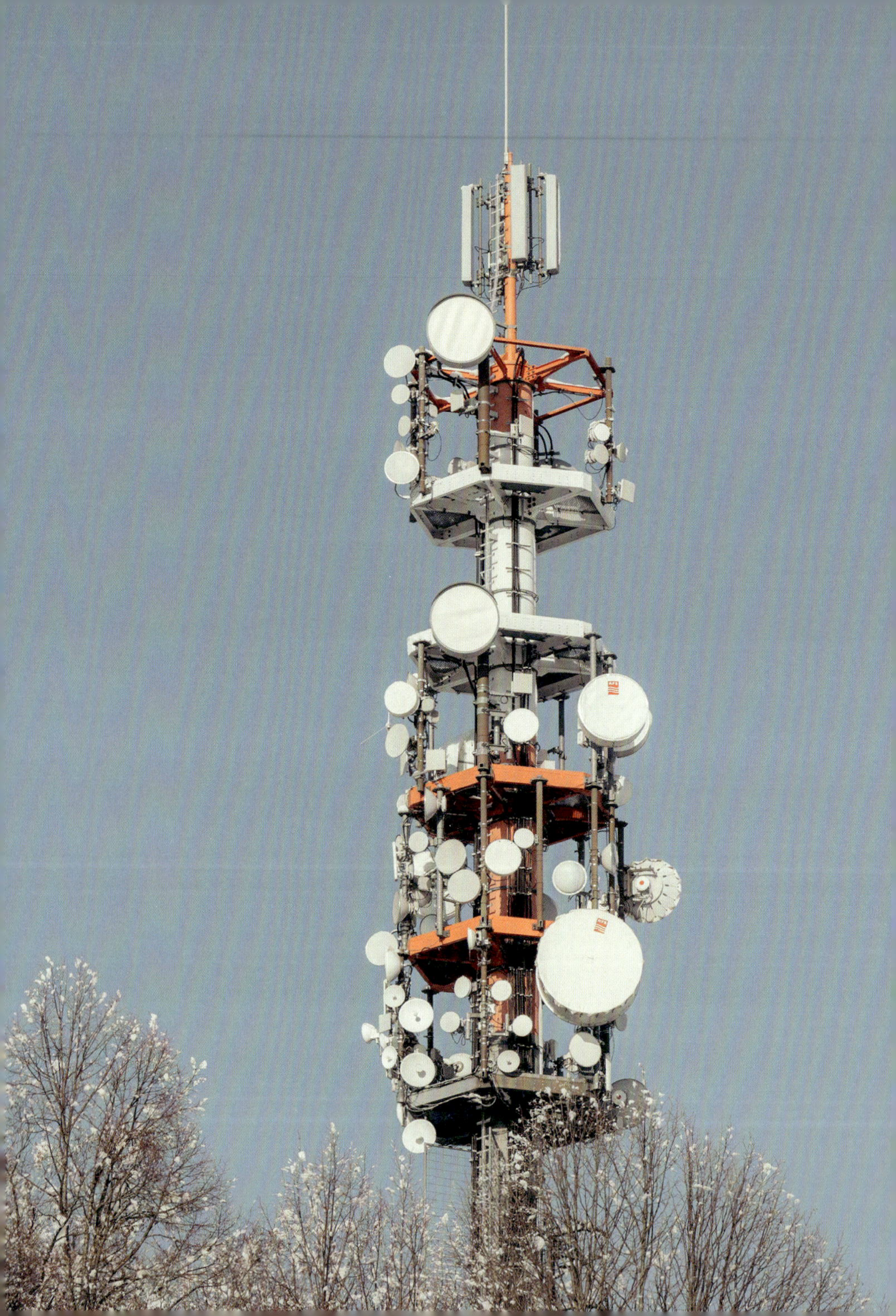

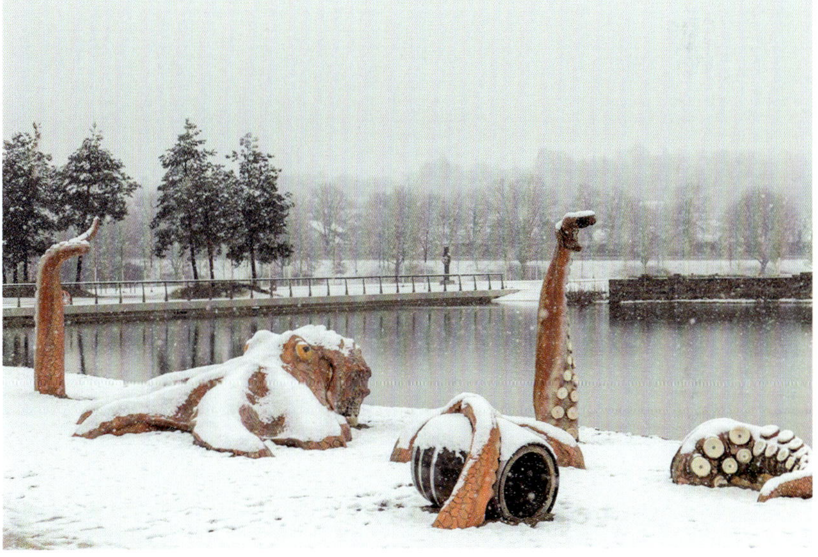

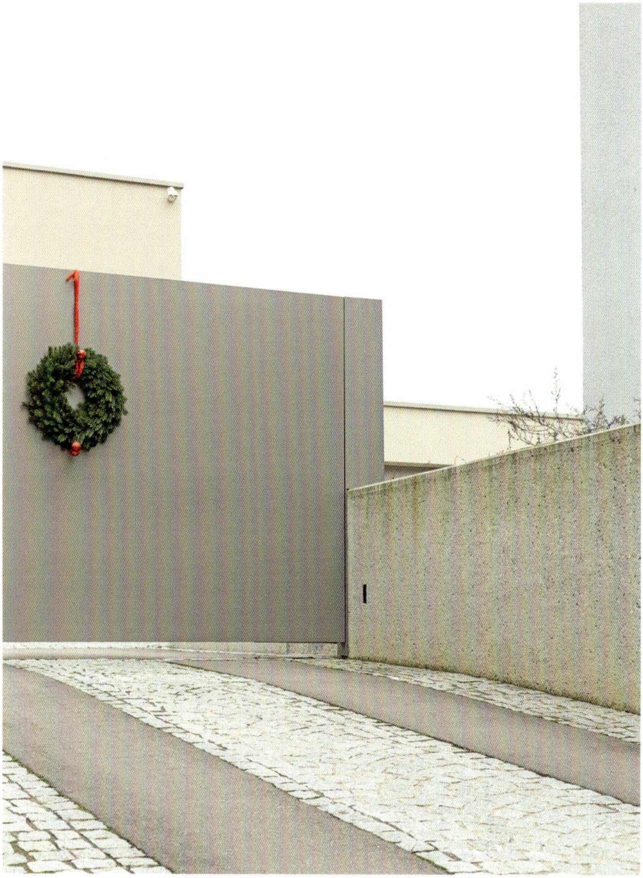

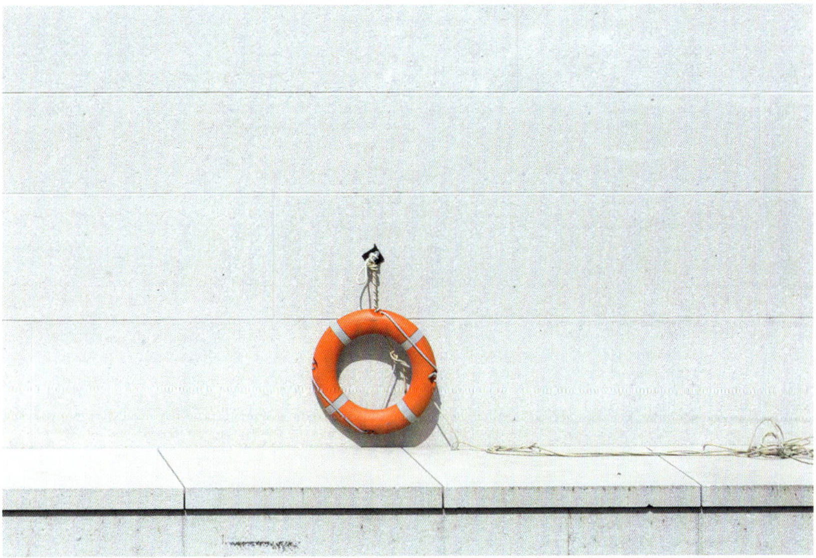

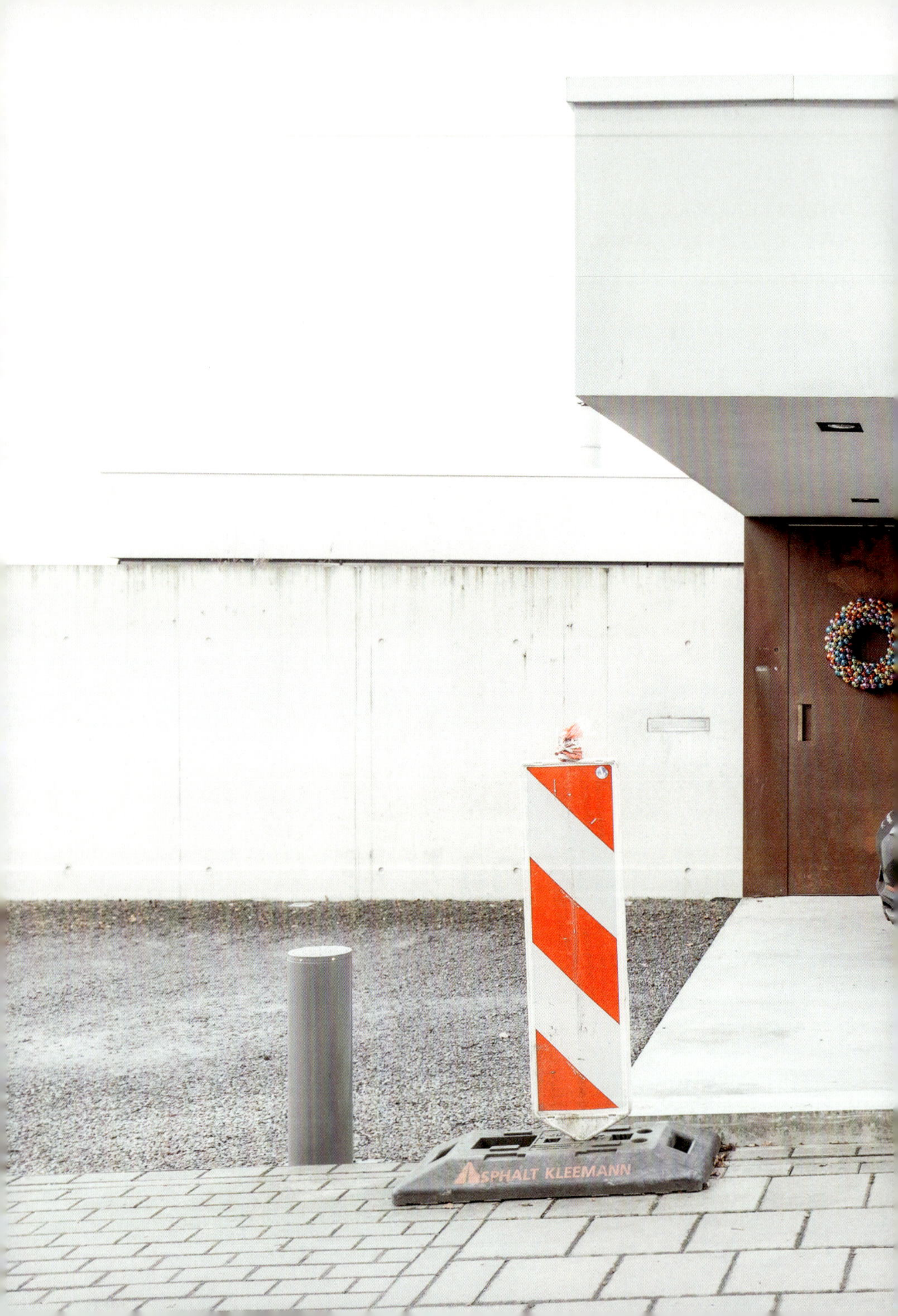
ASPHALT KLEEMANN

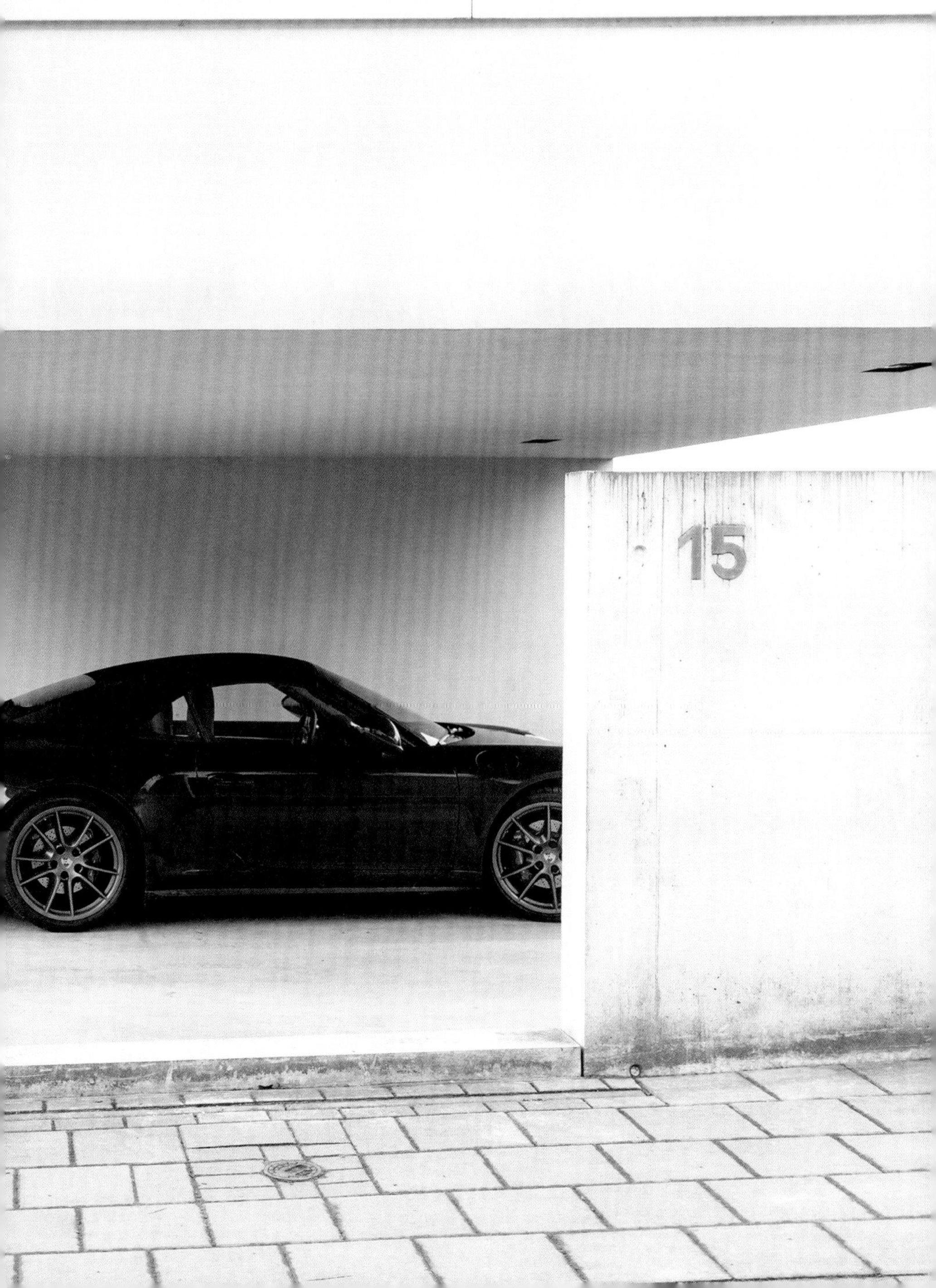
15

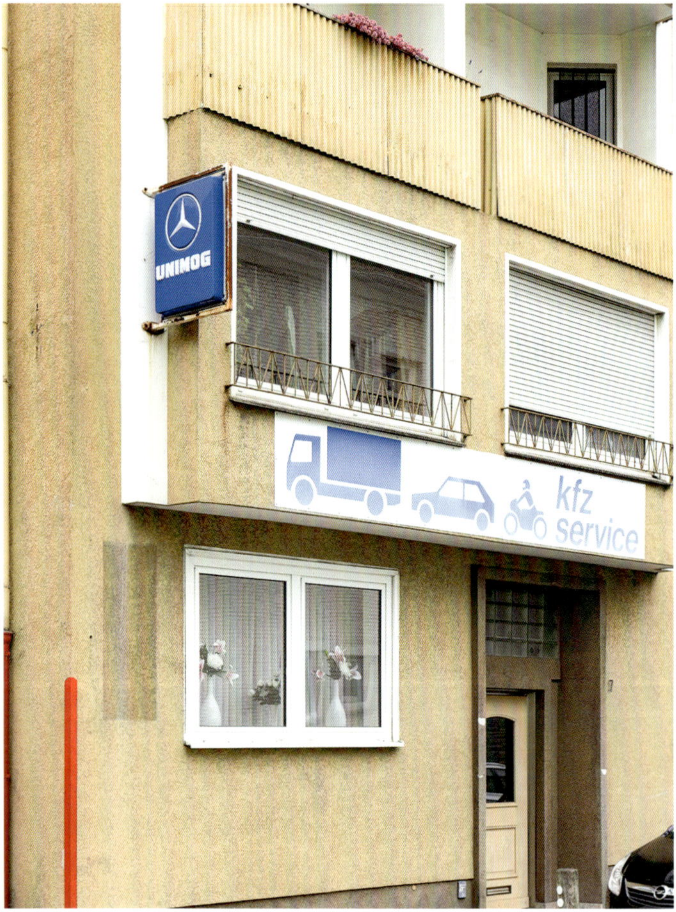
UNIMOG
kfz
service

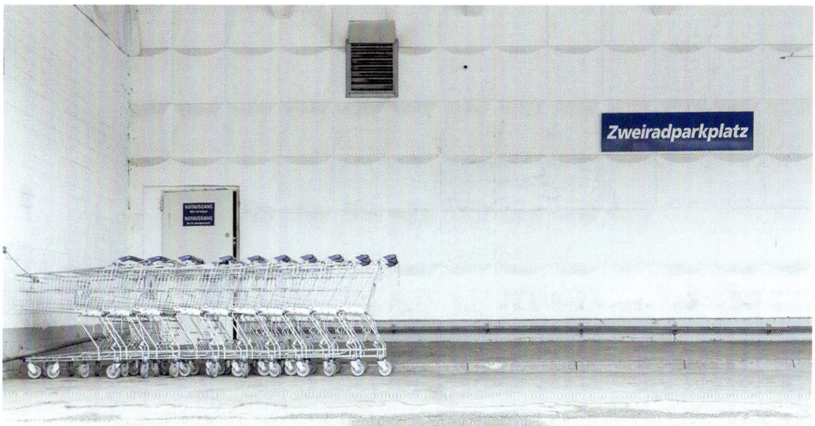
Zweiradparkplatz

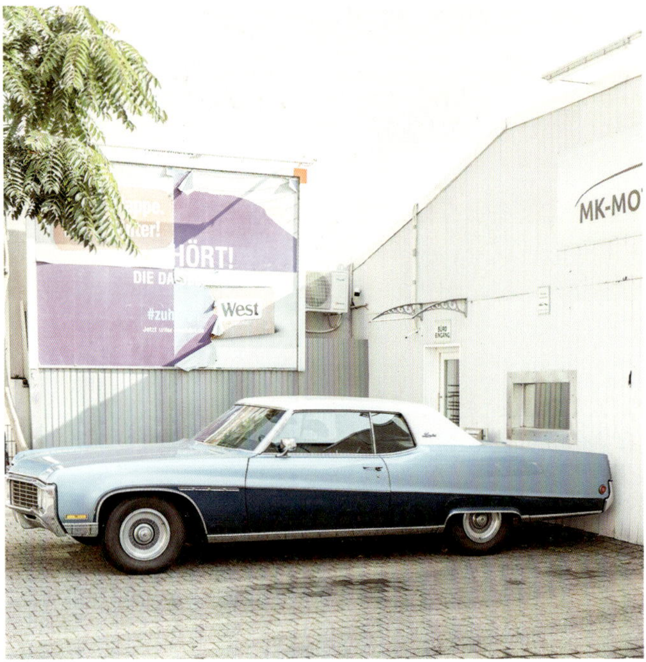
HÖRT!
West
MK-MO

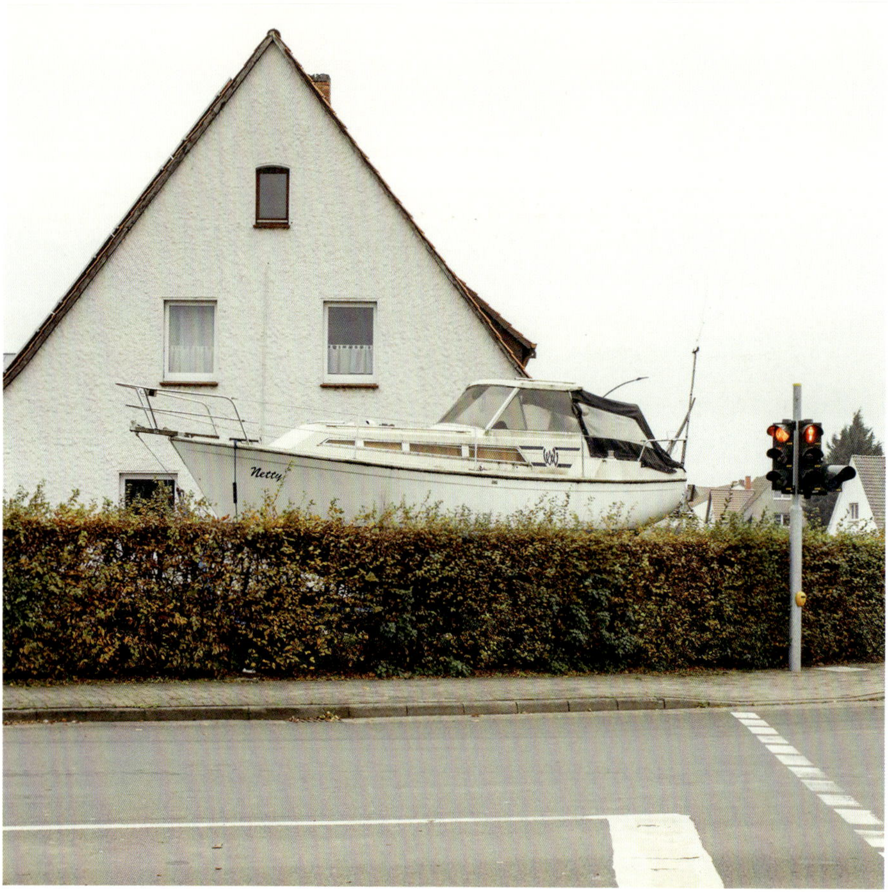
Netty

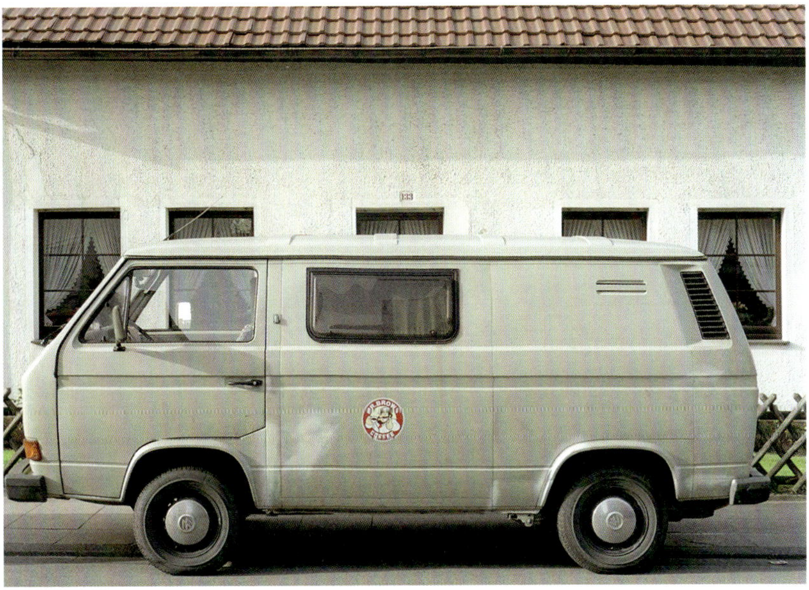

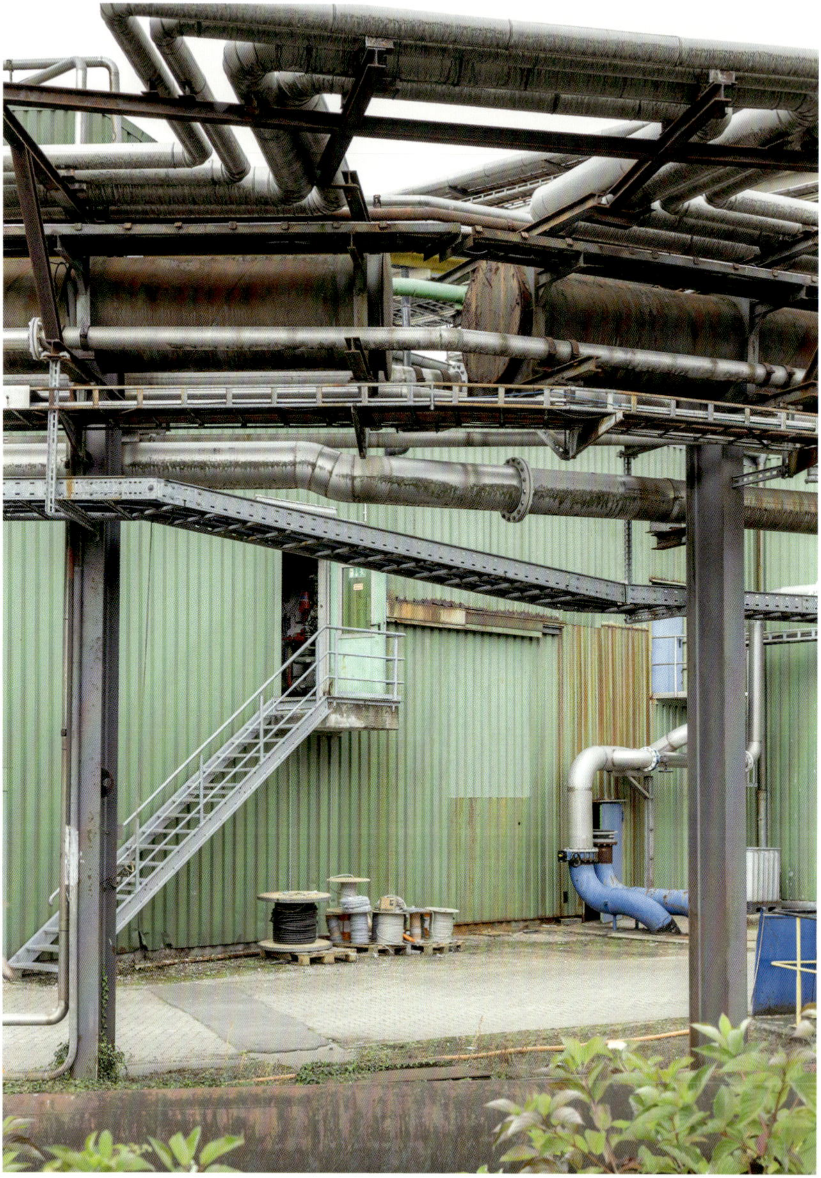

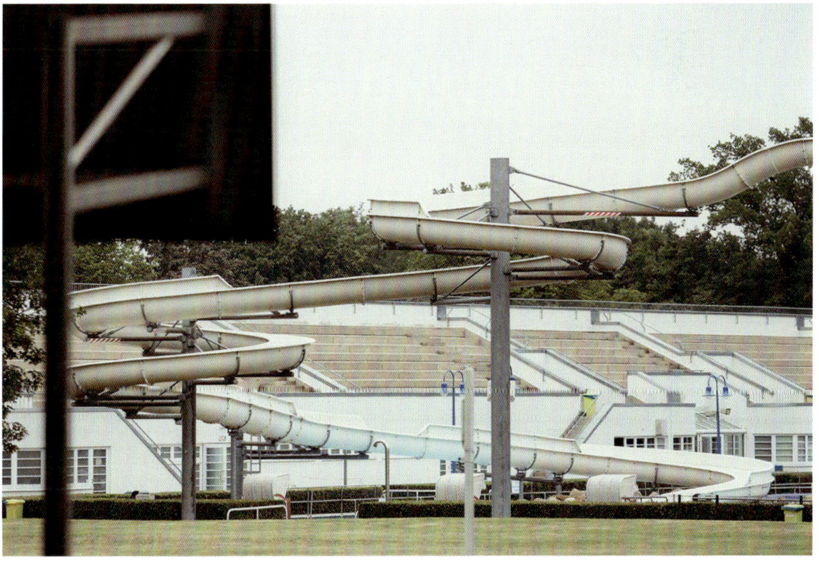

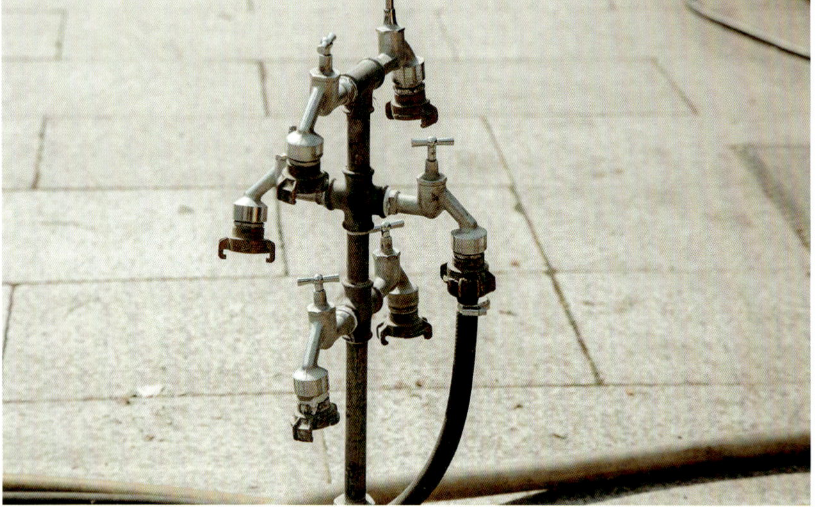

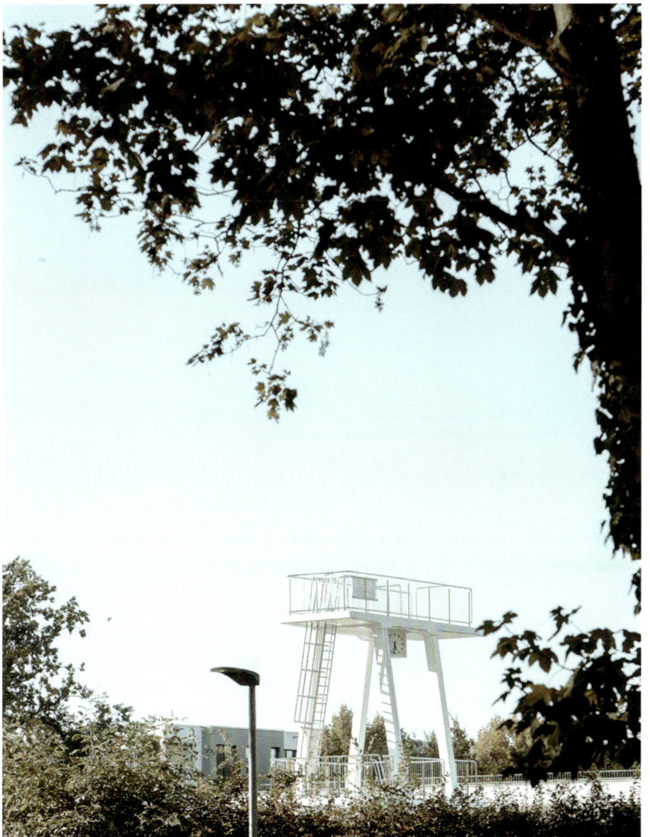

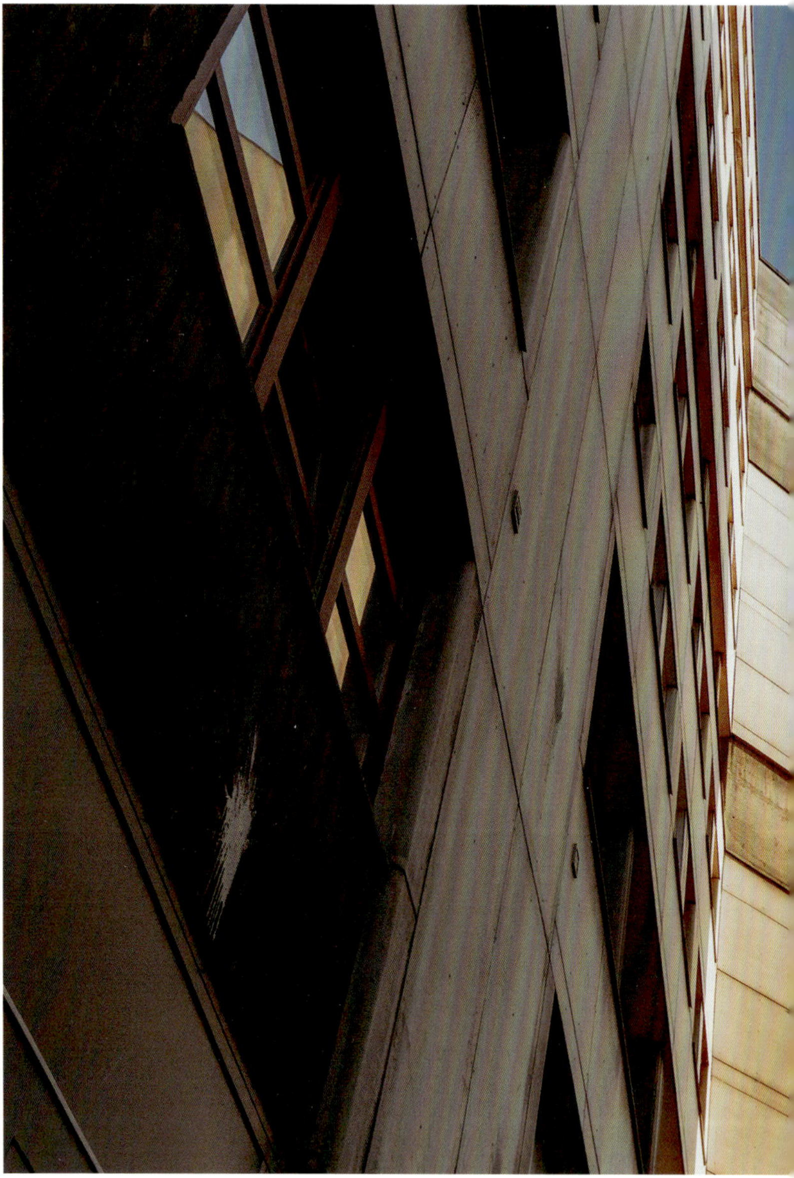

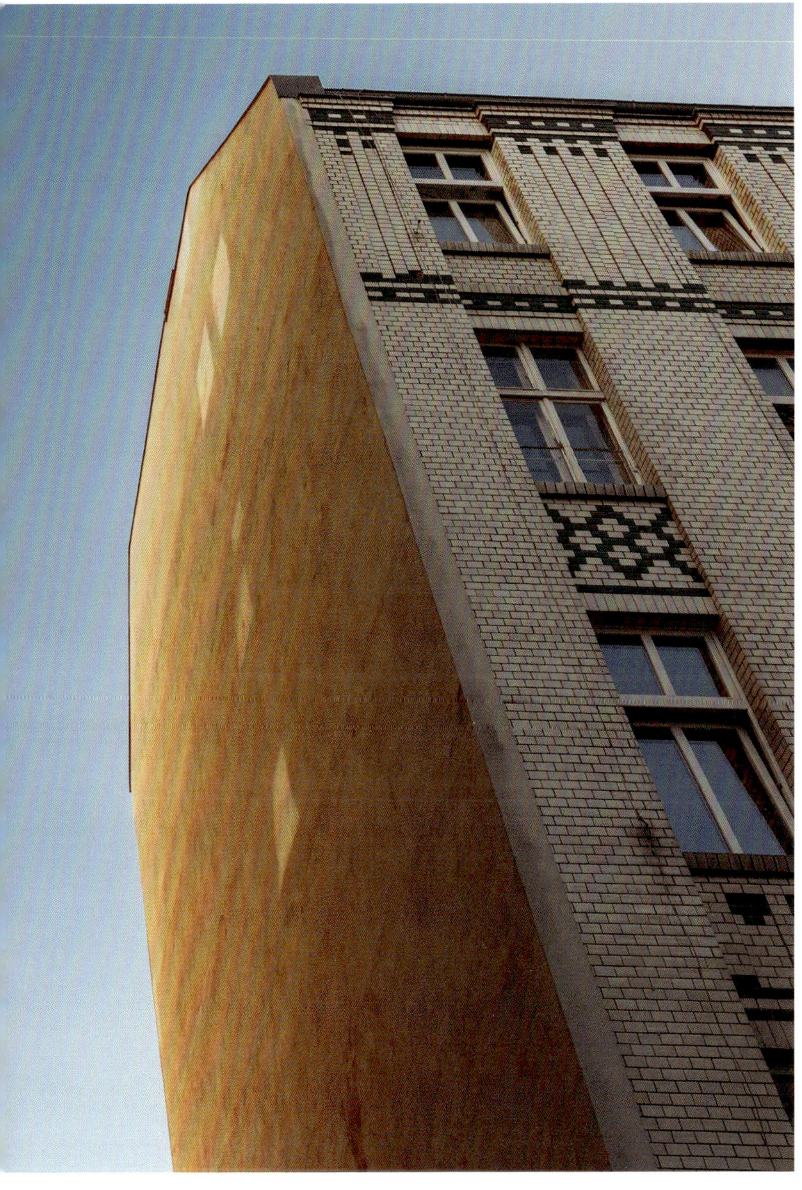

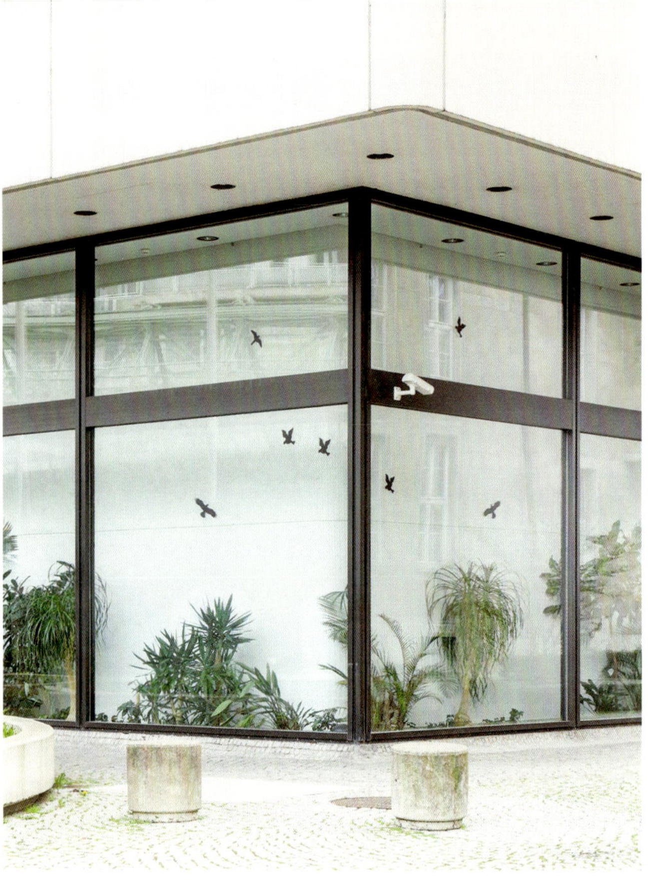

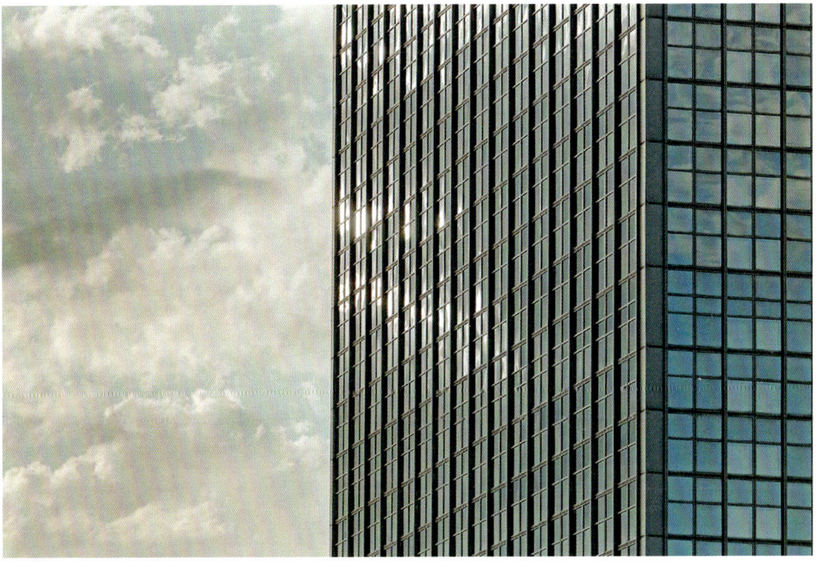

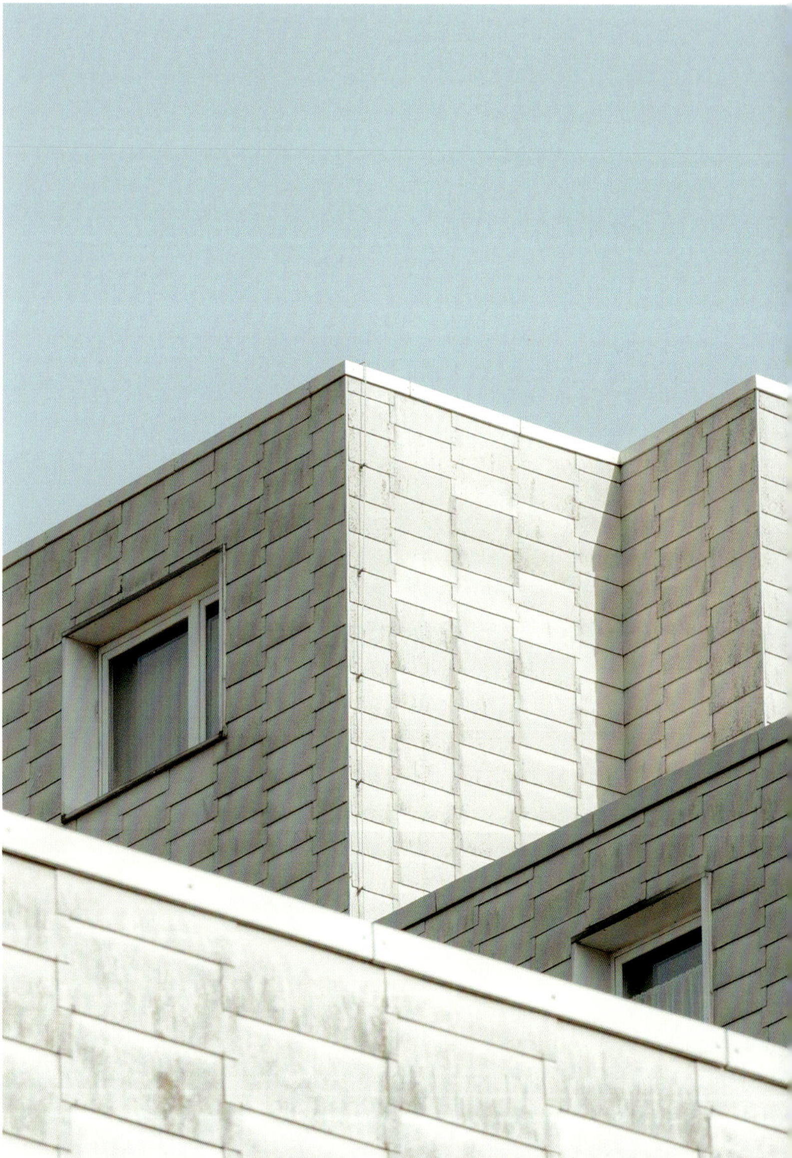

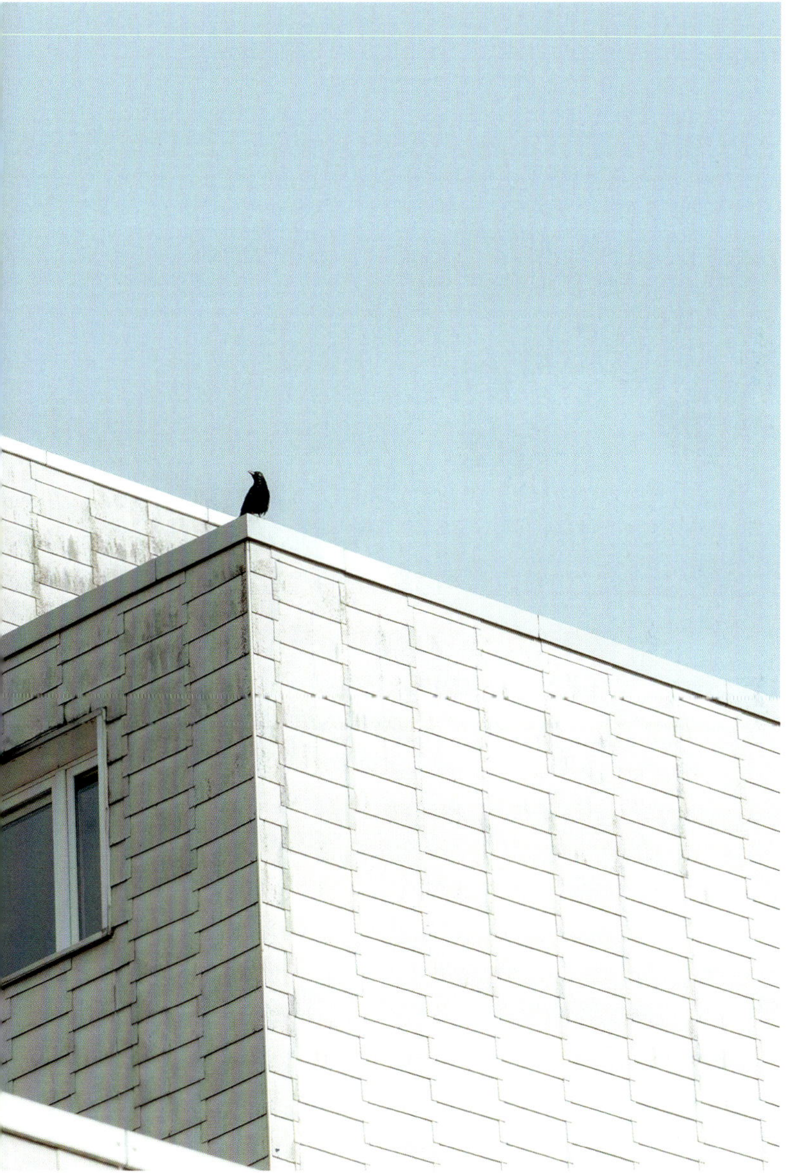

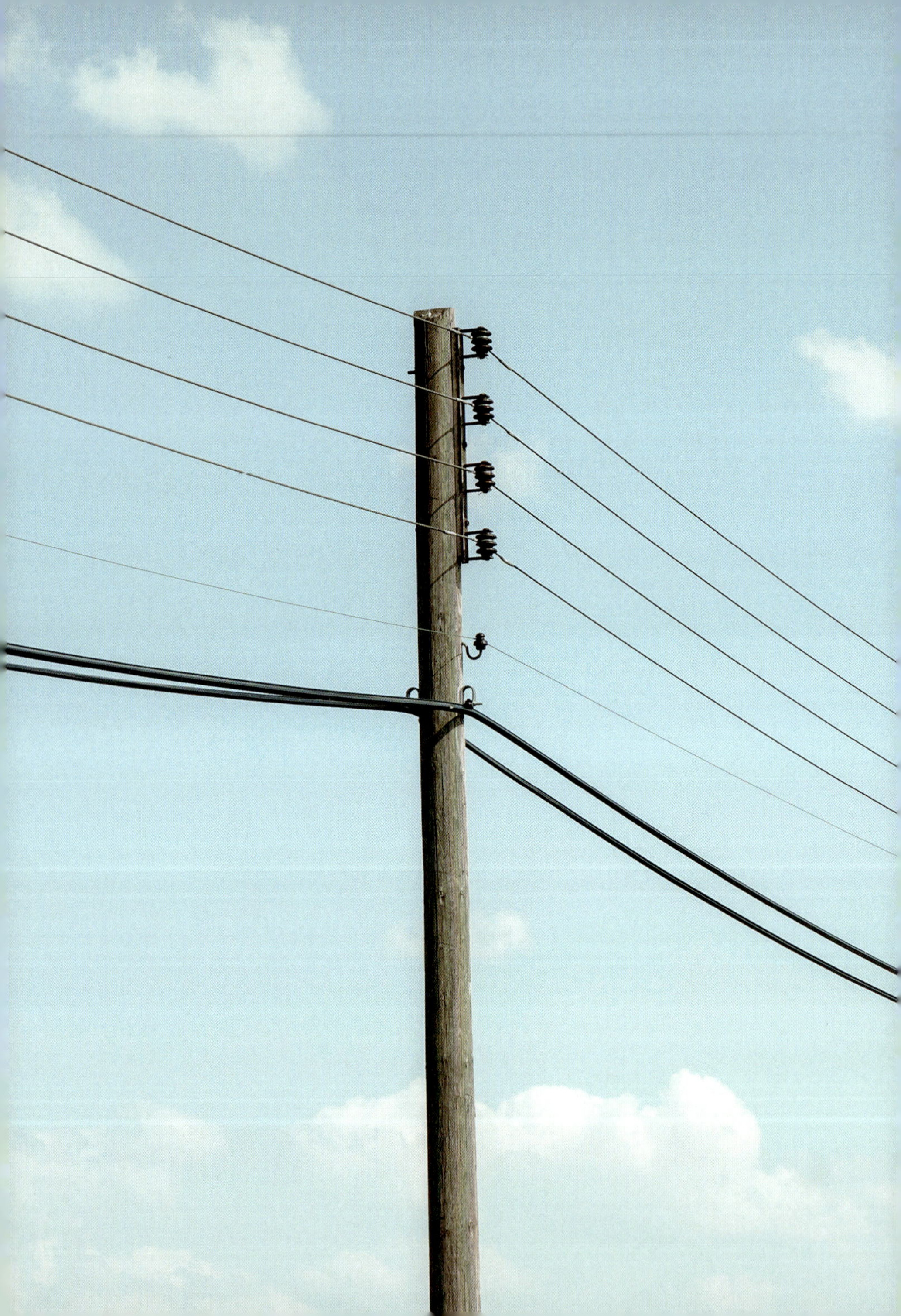

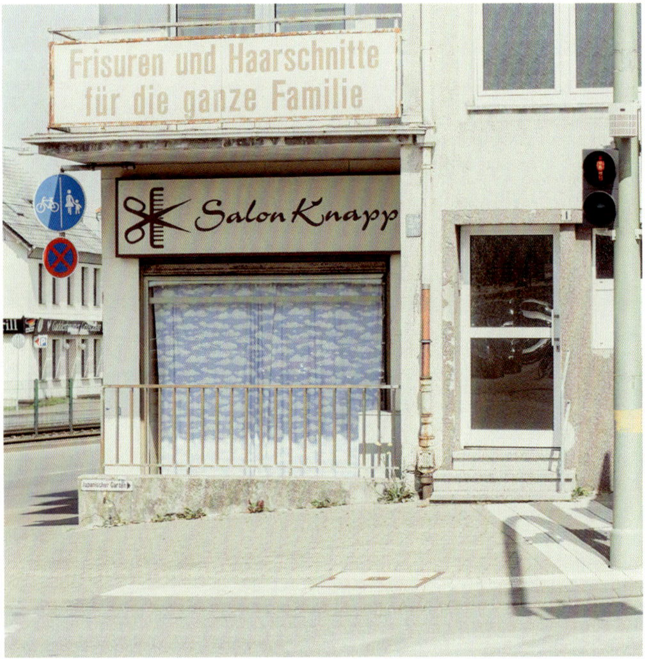
Frisuren und Haarschnitte
für die ganze Familie
Salon Knapp

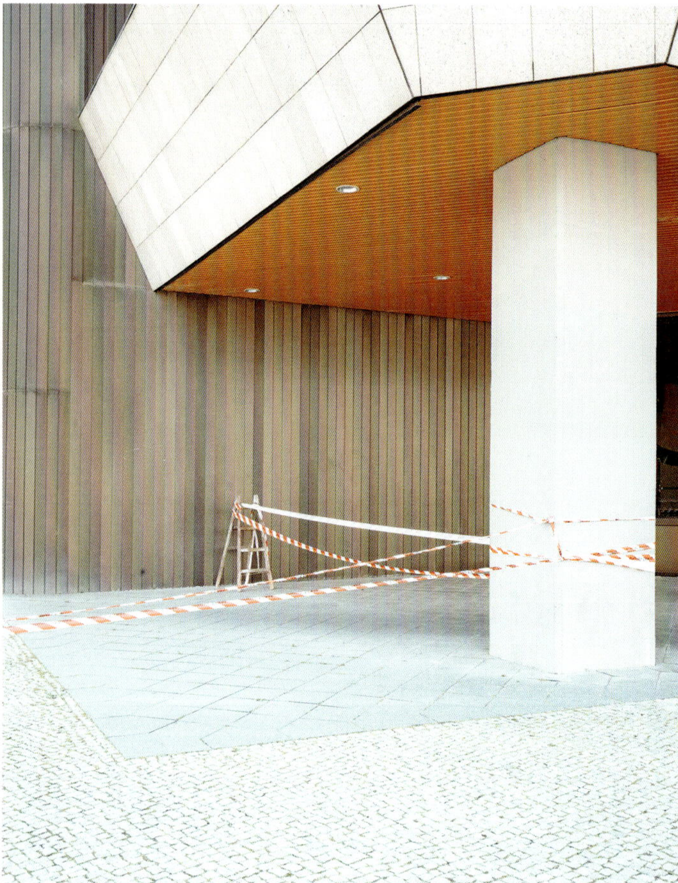

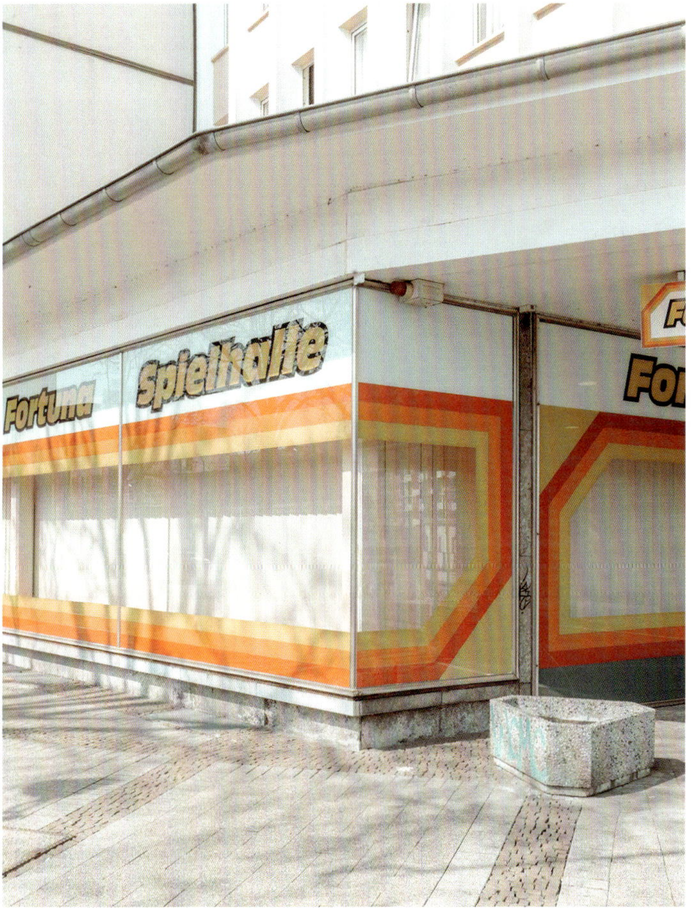
Fortuna
Spielhalle
Fo

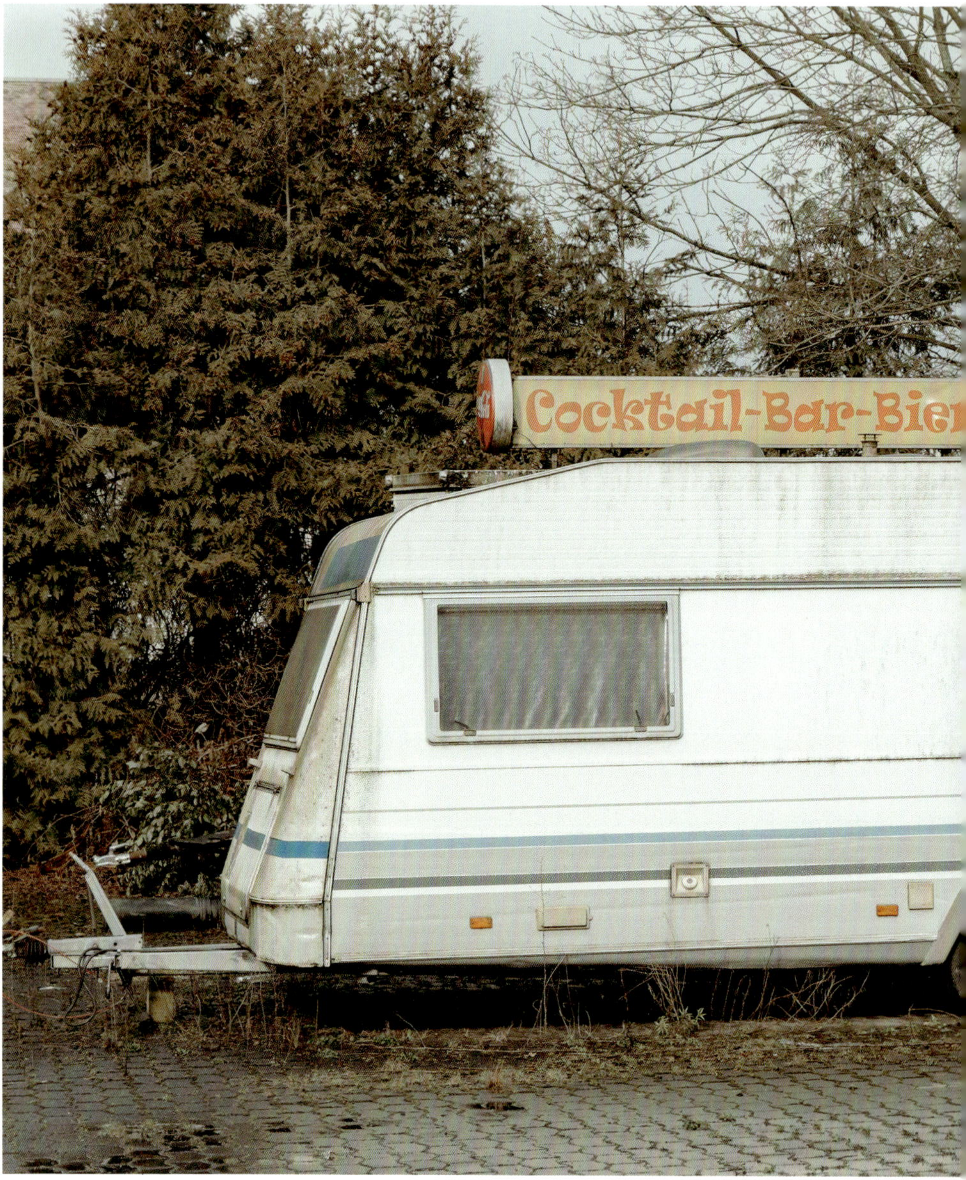
Cocktail-Bar-Bier

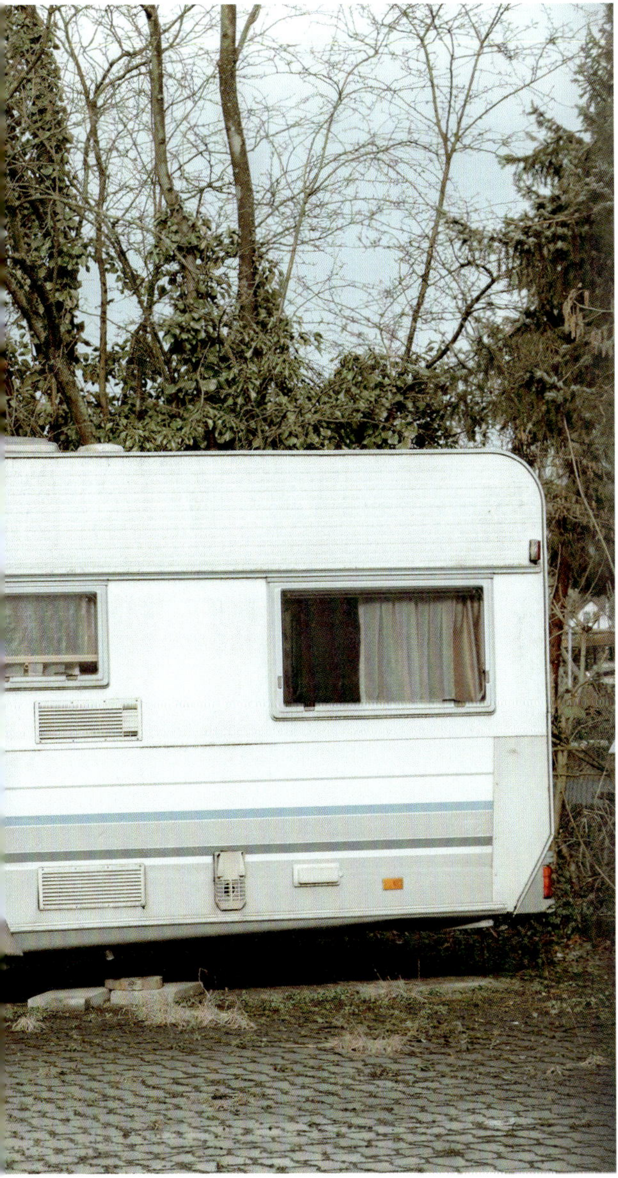

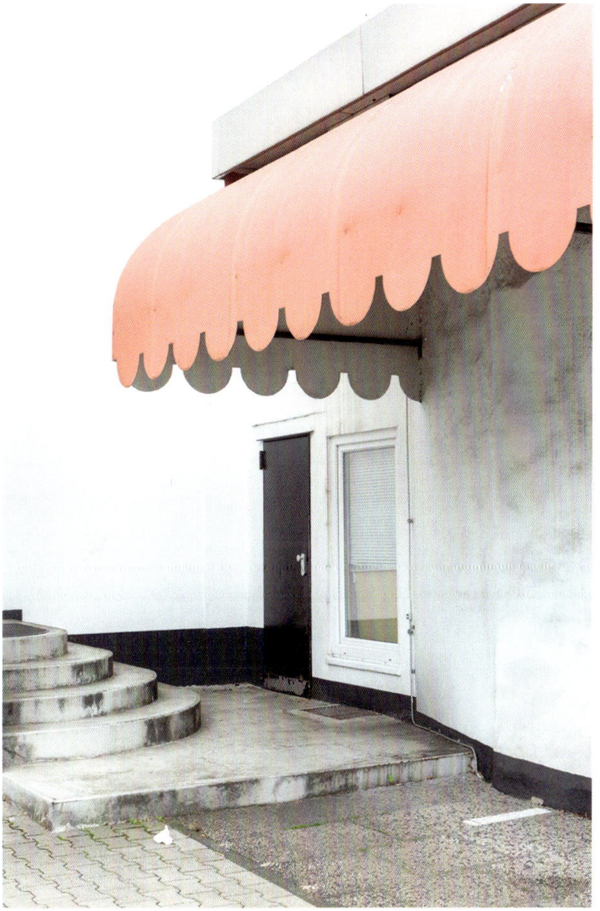

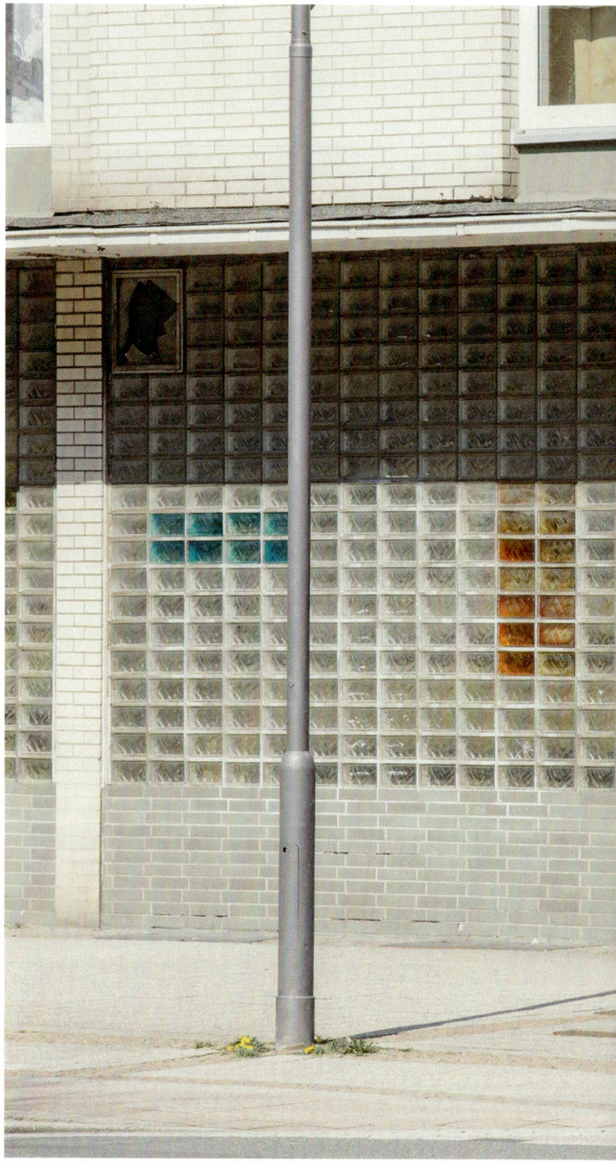

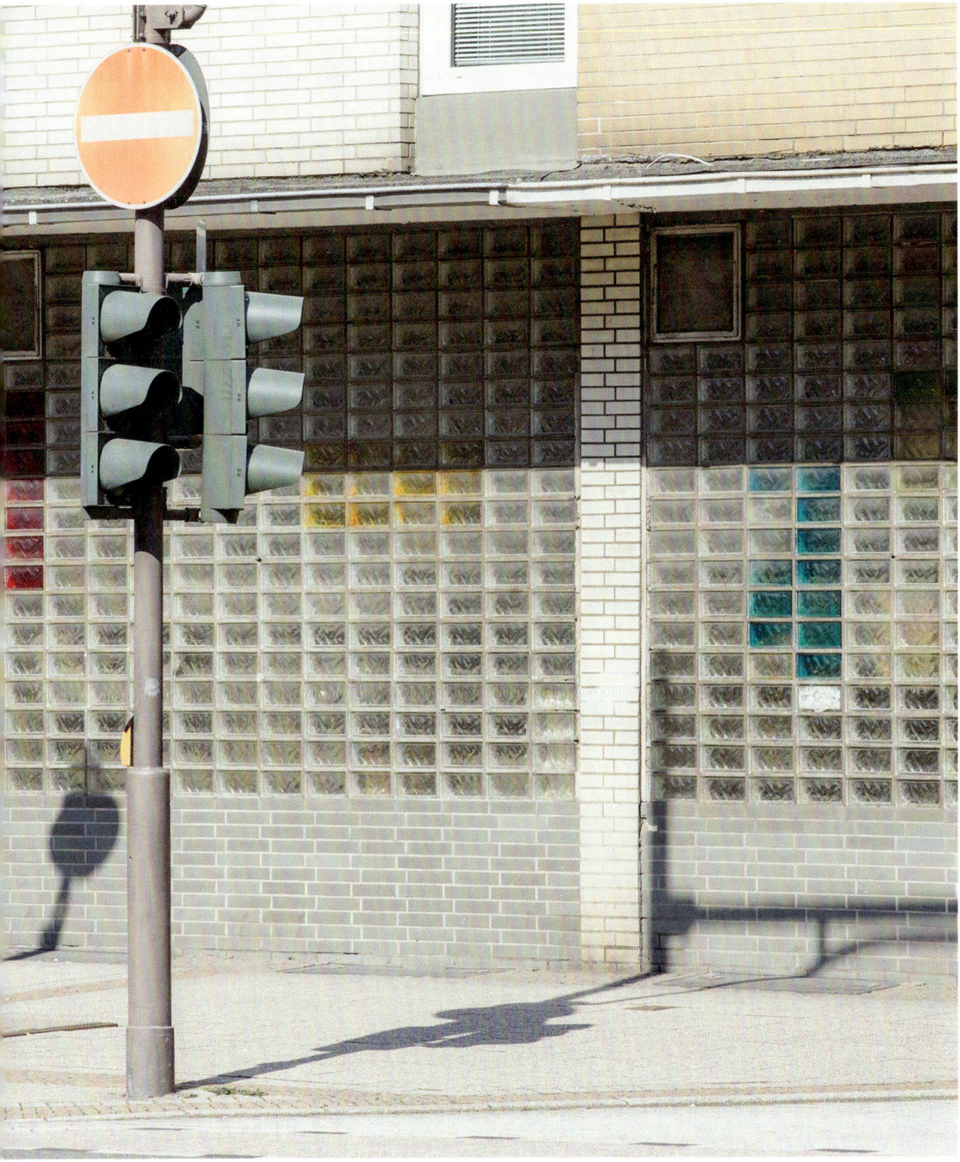

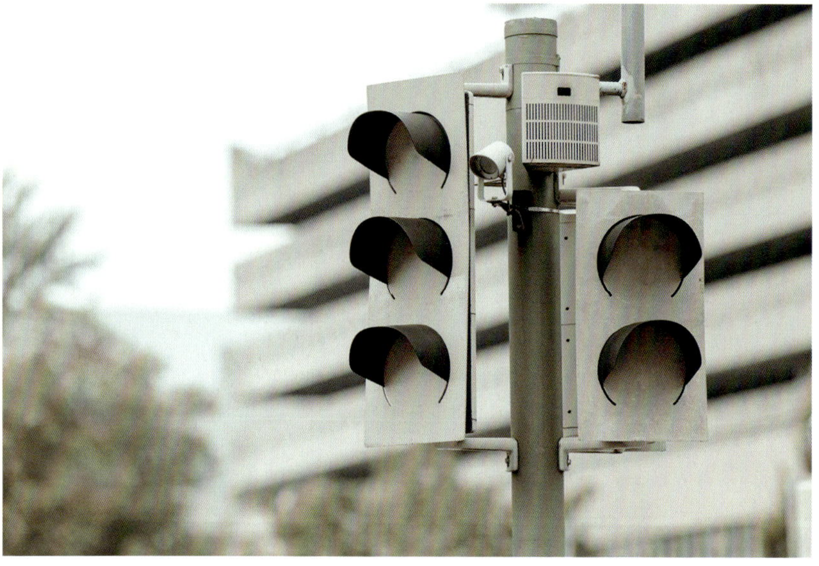

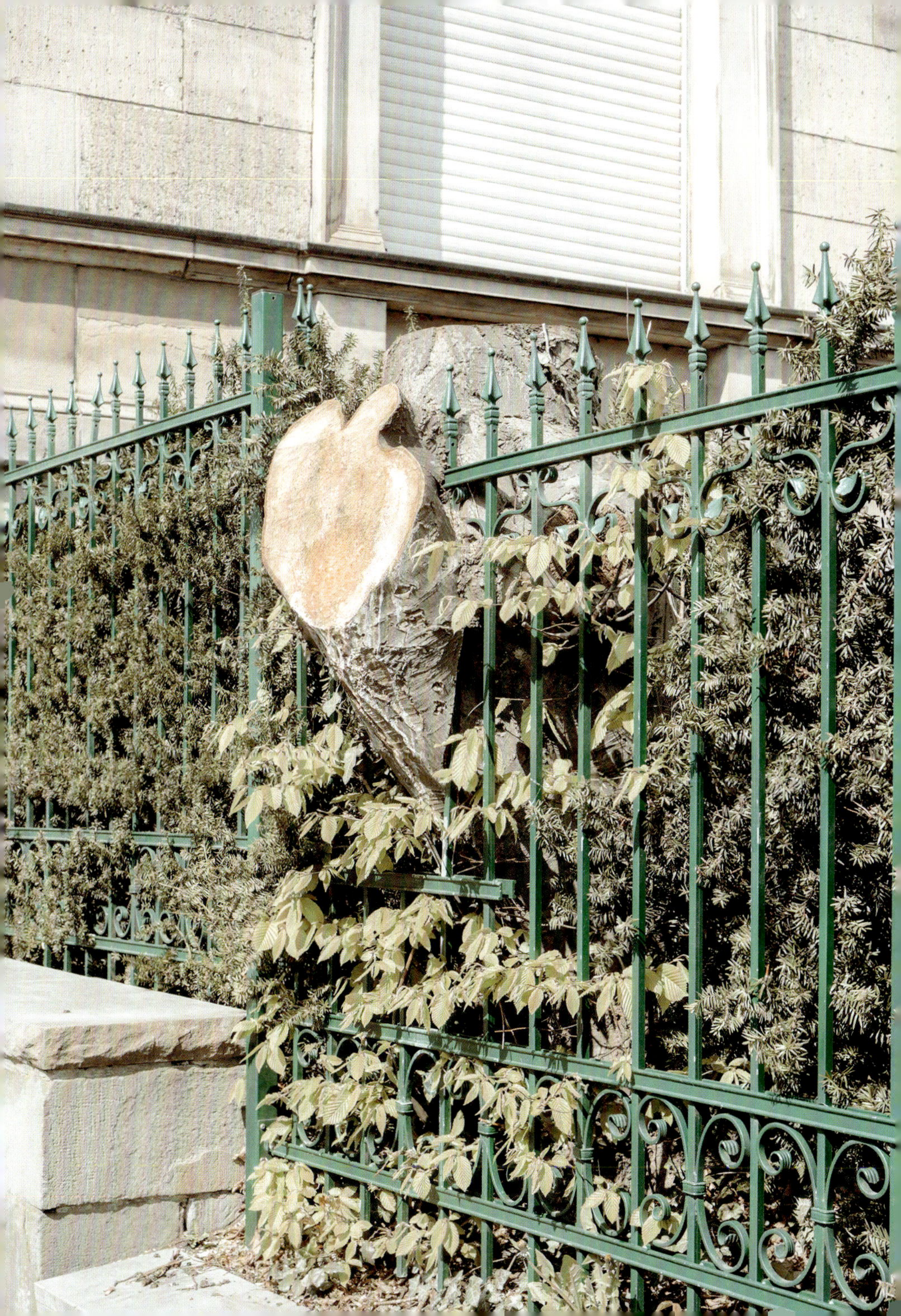

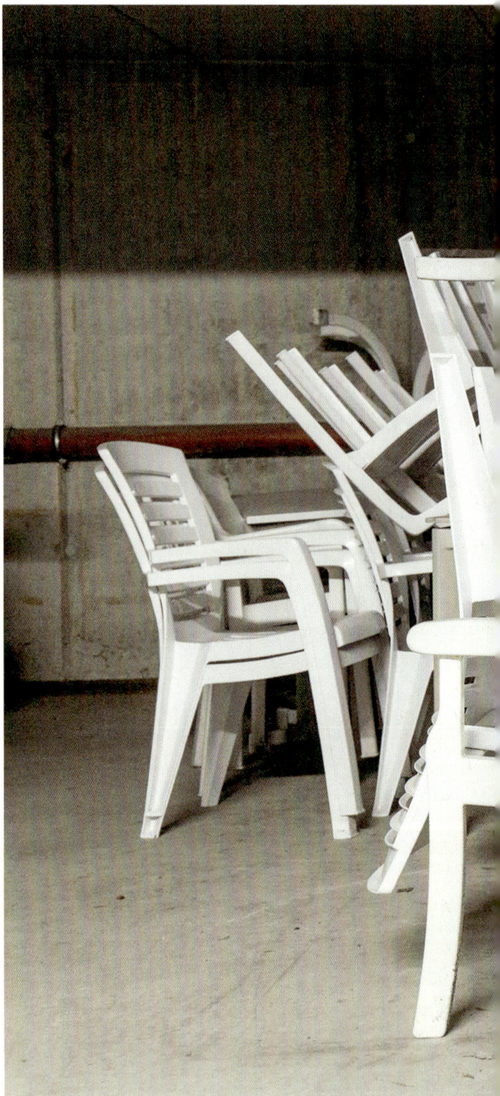

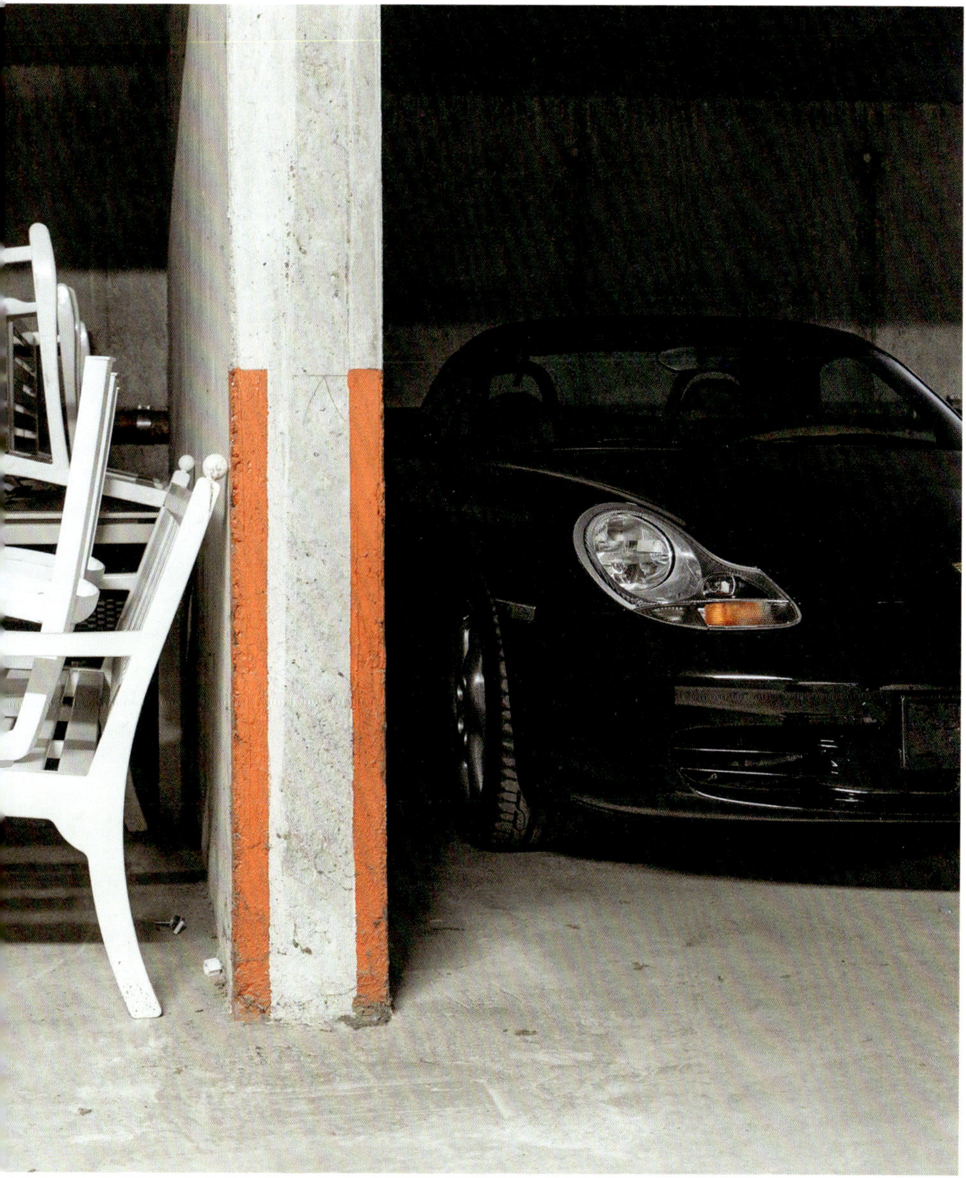

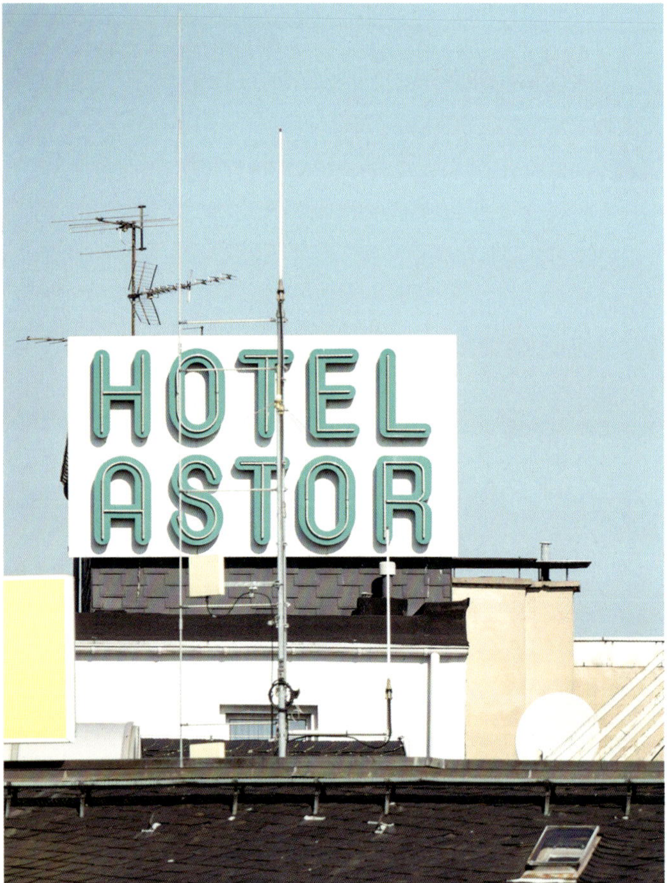
HOTEL
ASTOR

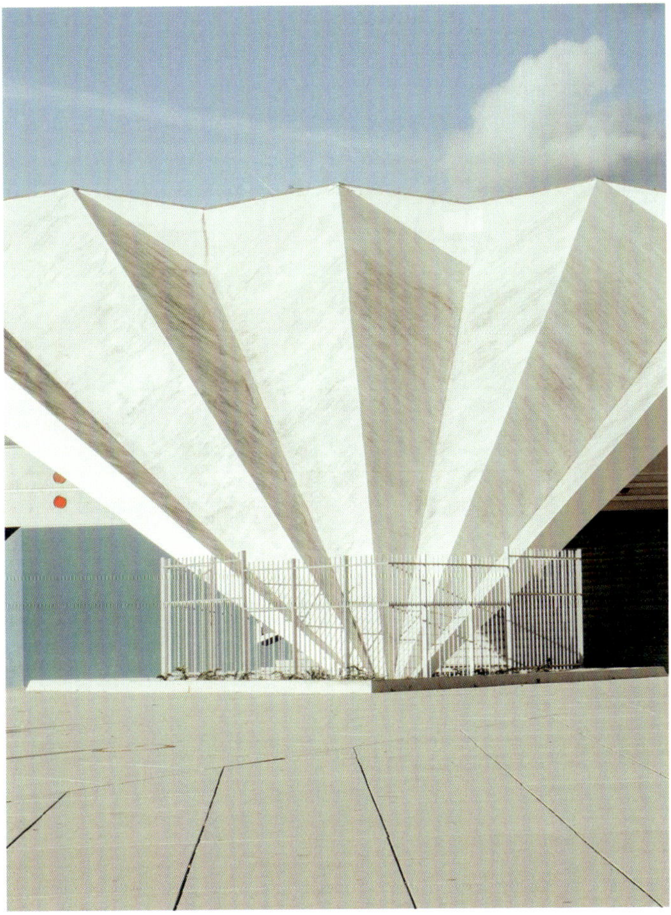

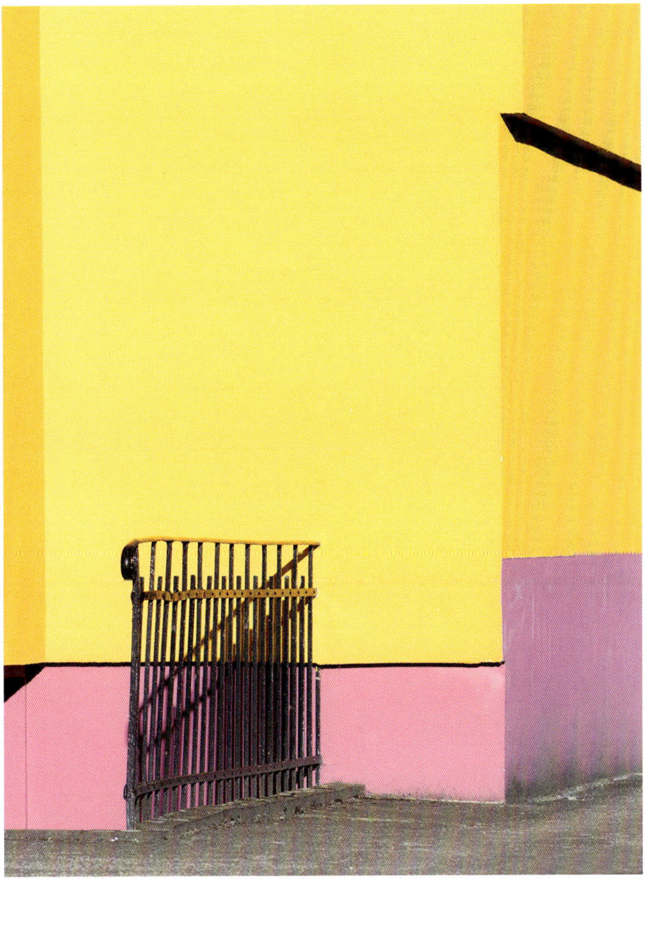

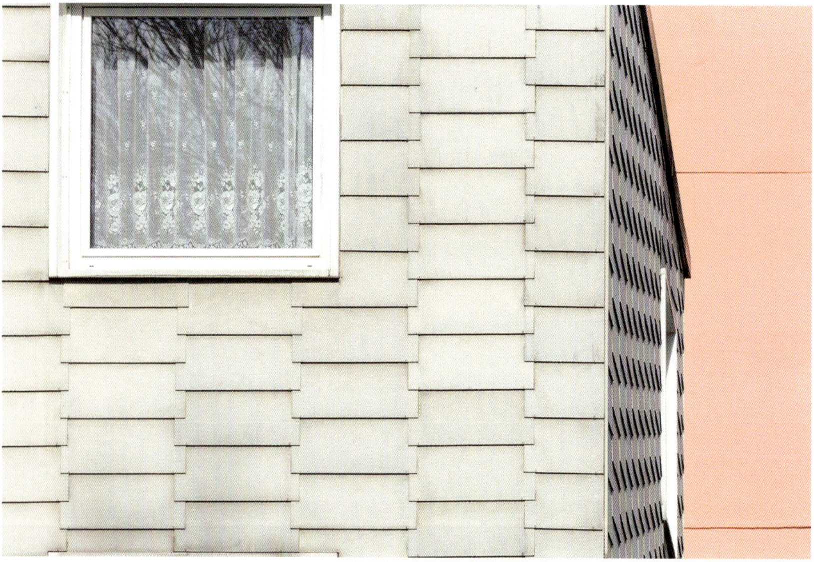

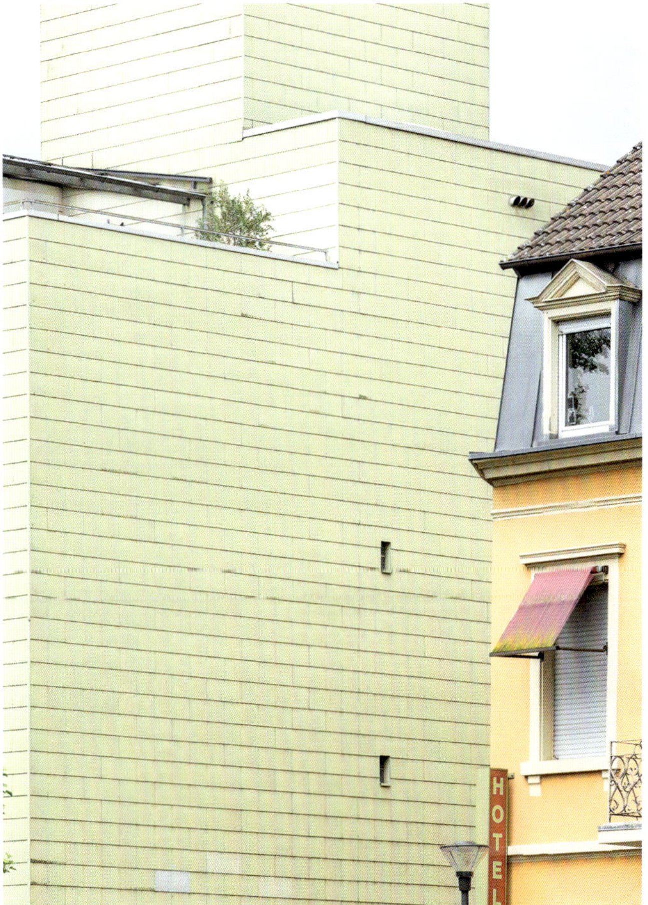
HOTEL

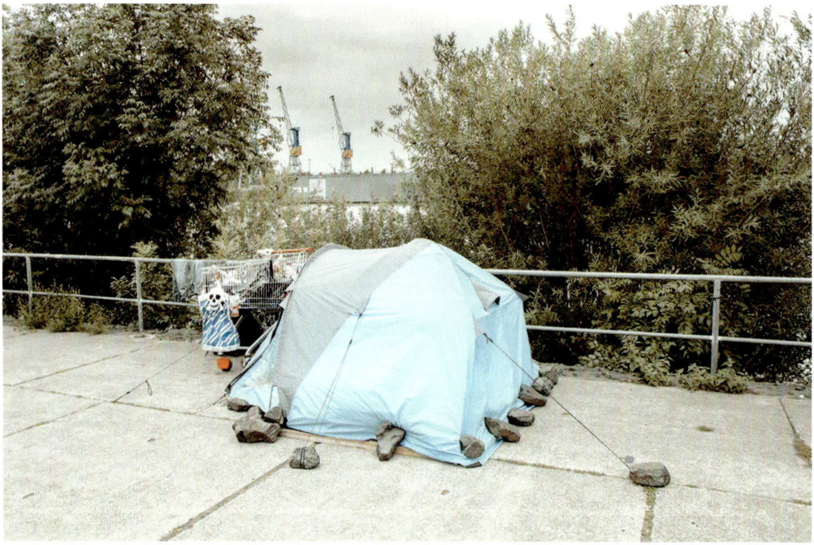

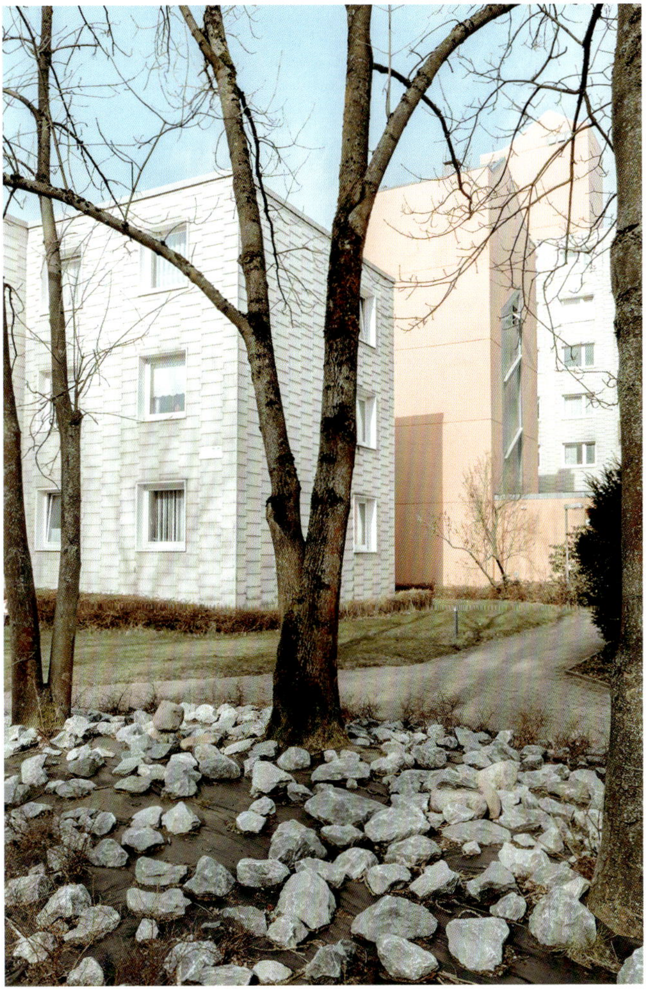

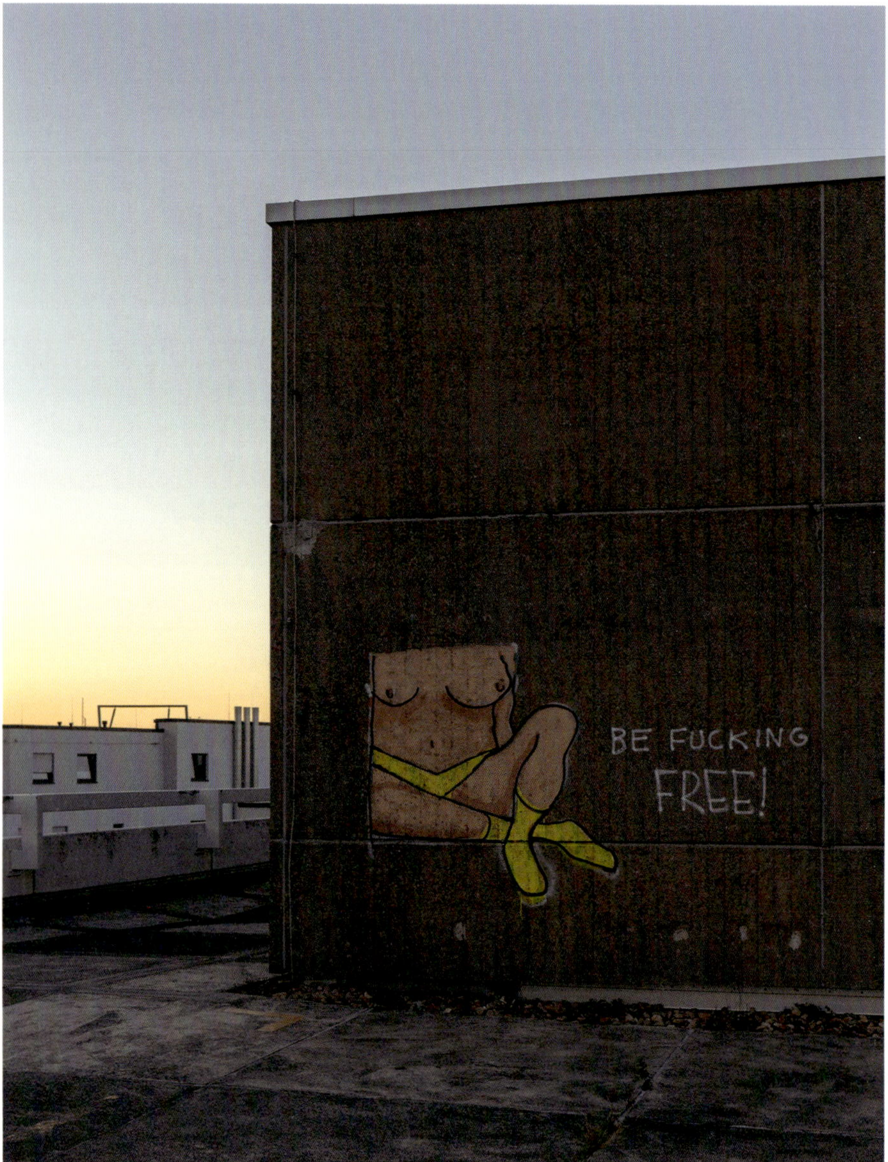
BE FUCKING
FREE!

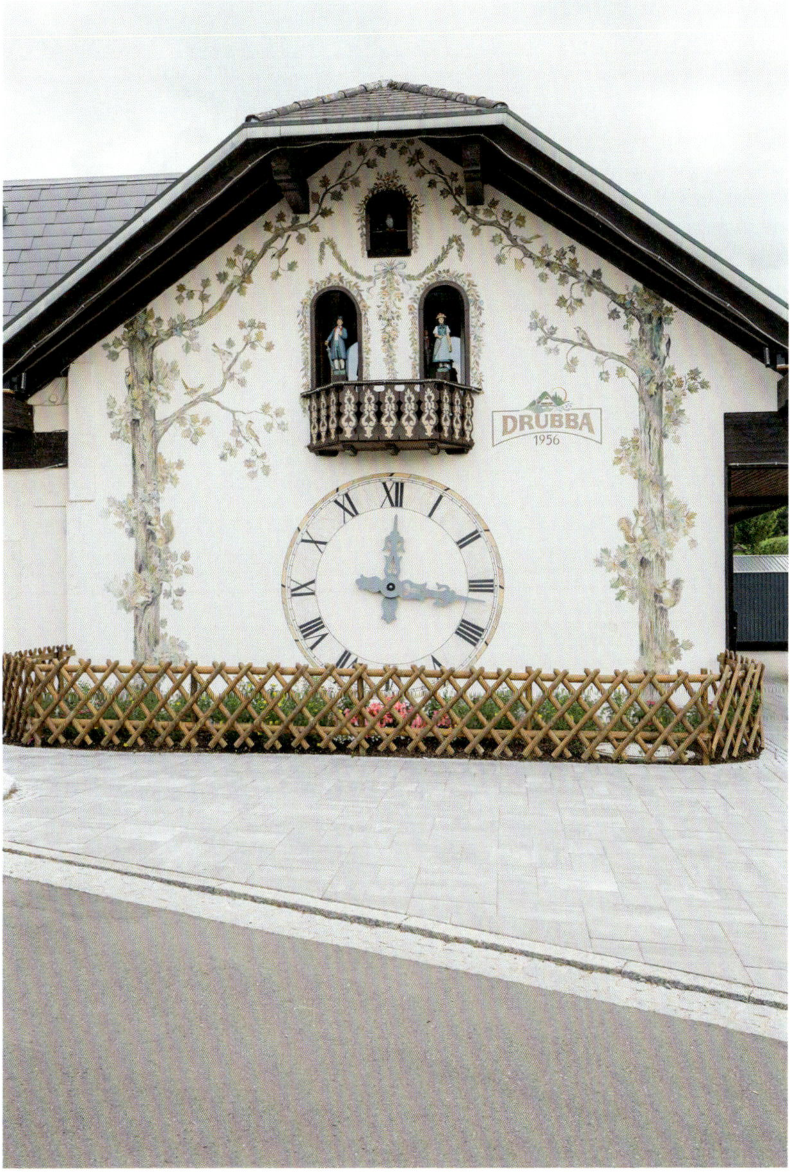
DRUBBA
1956

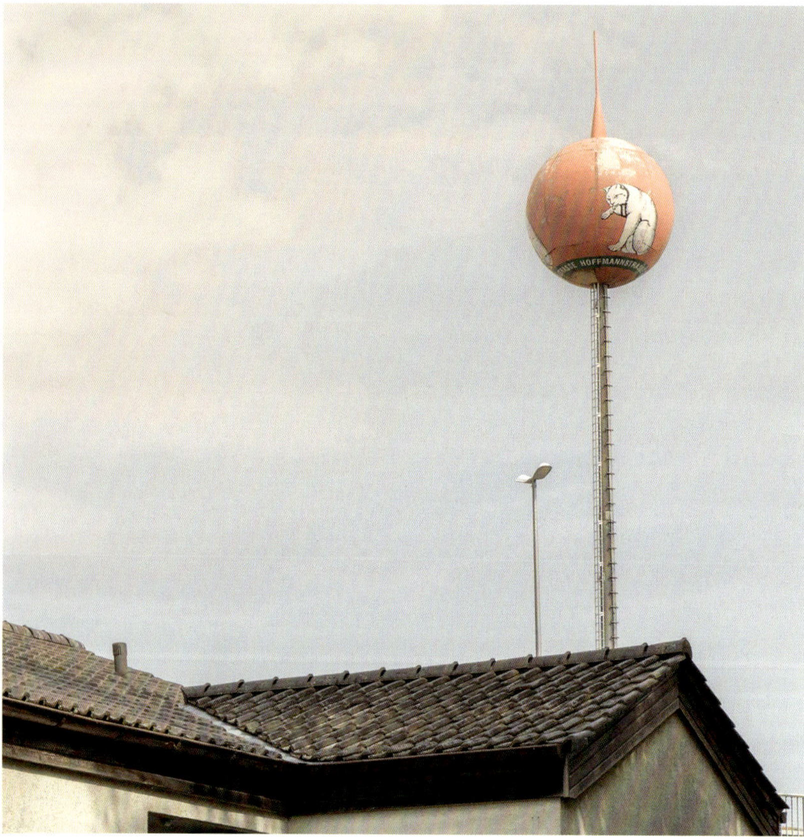

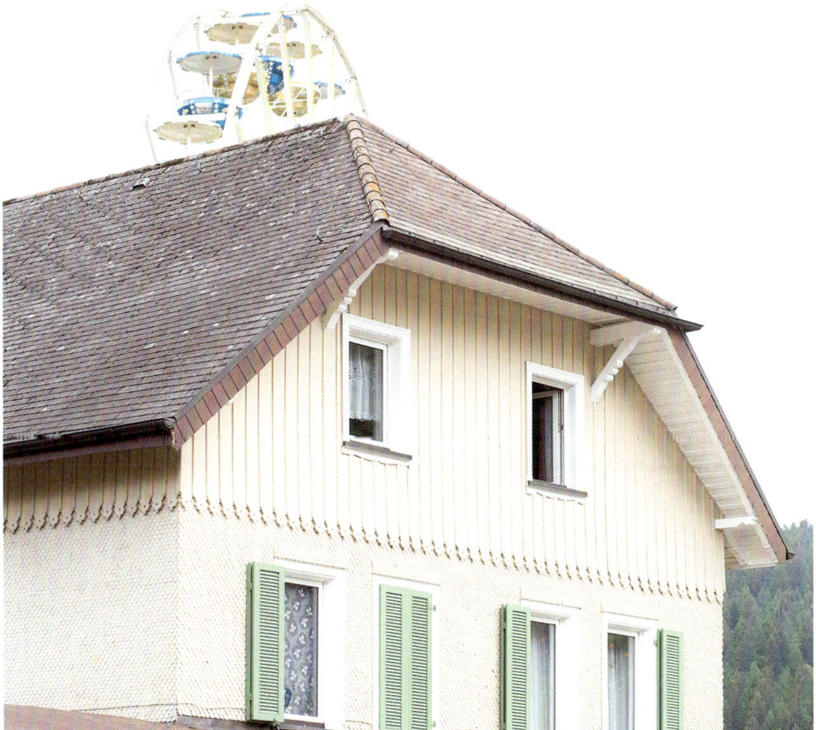

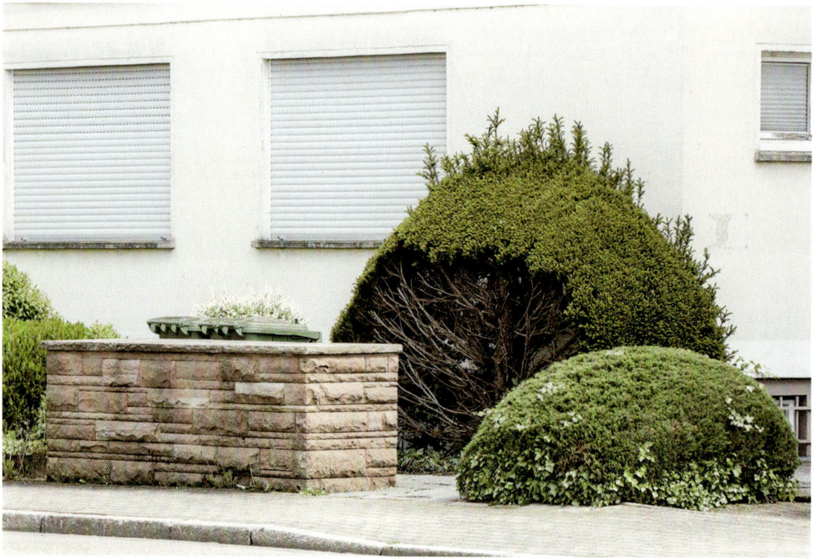

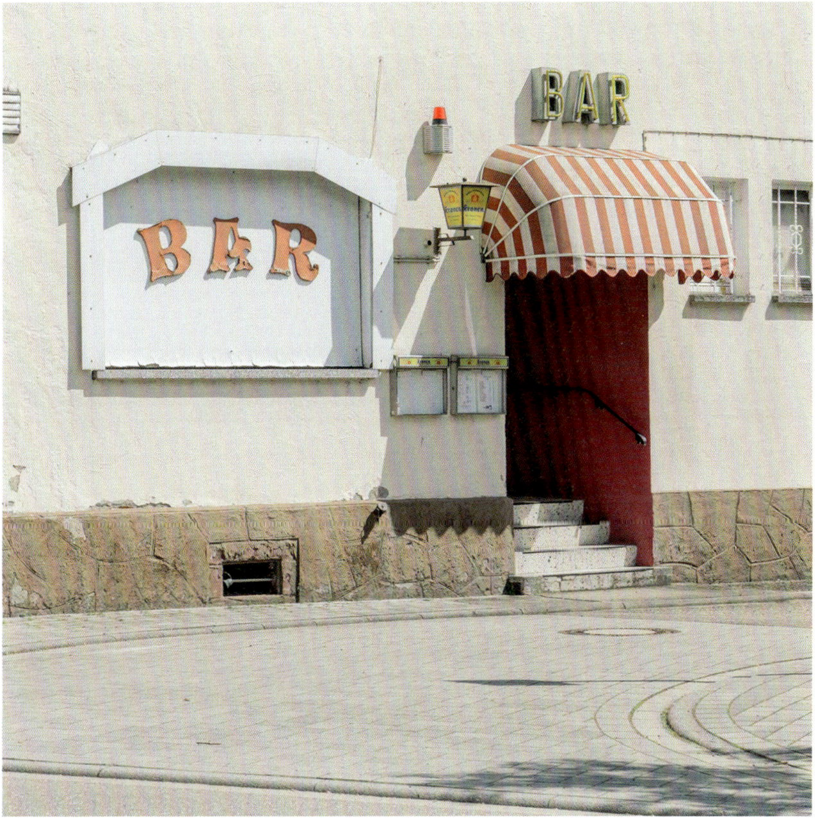
BAR
BAR

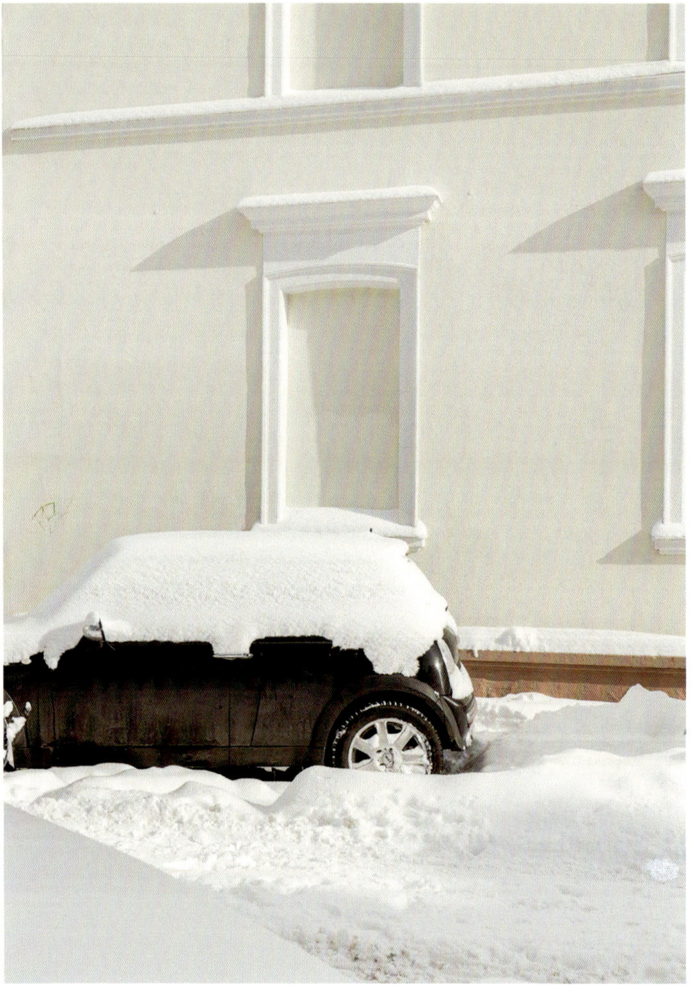

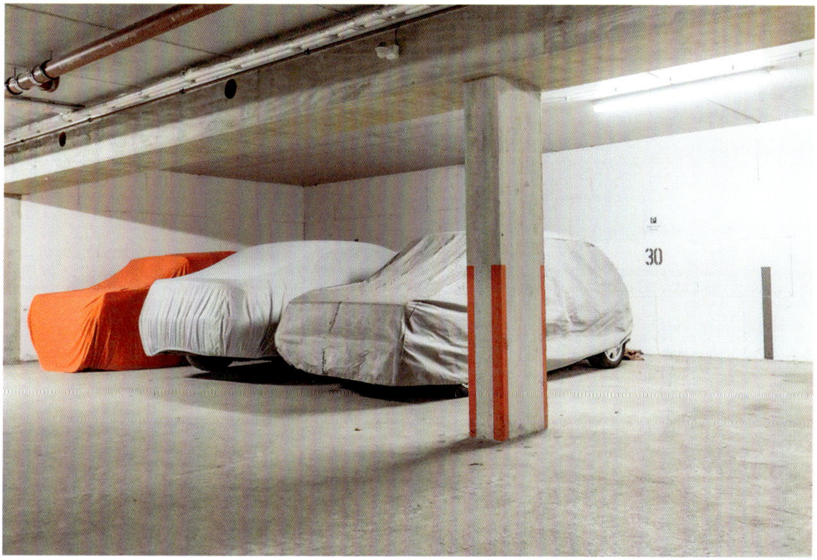
30

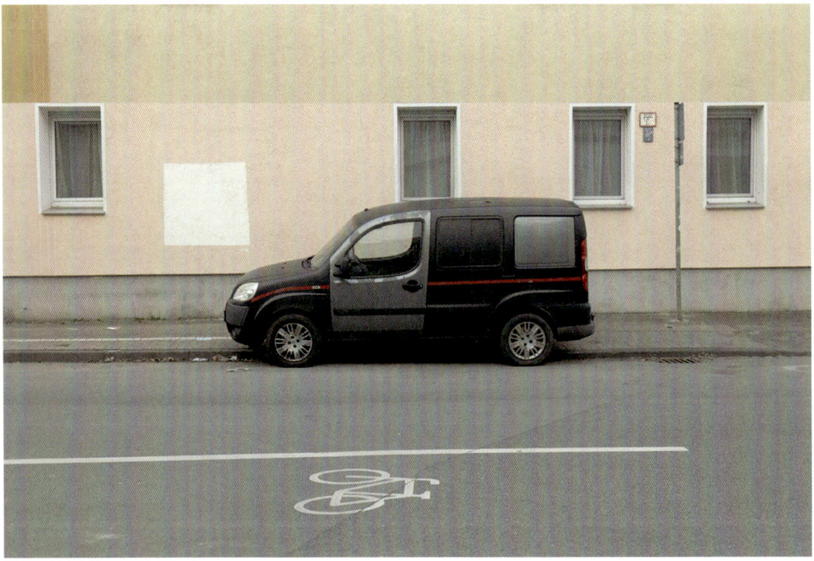

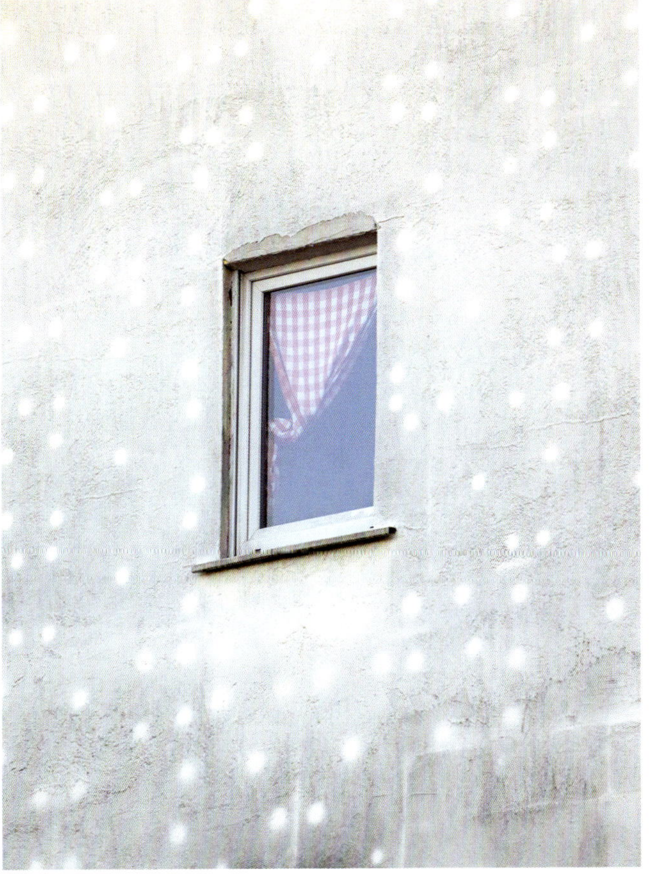

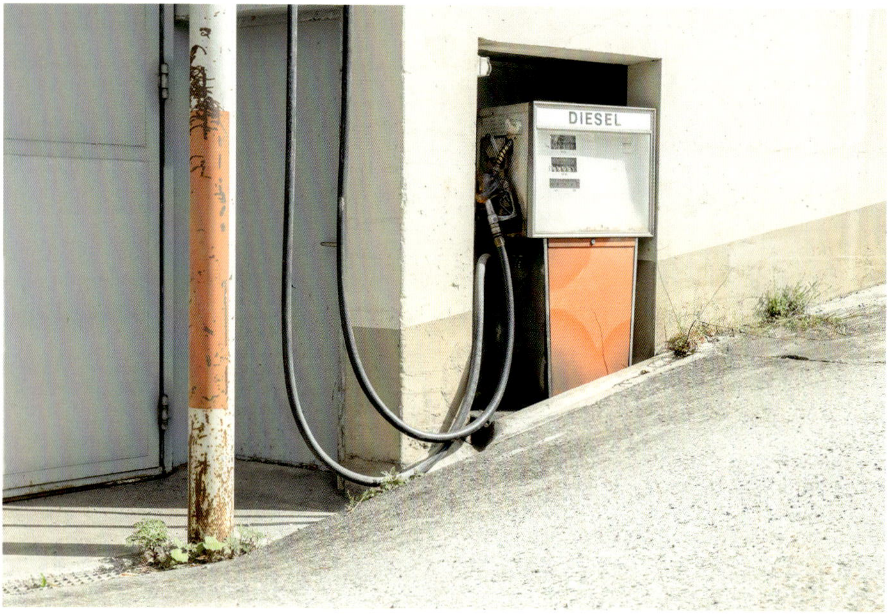
DIESEL

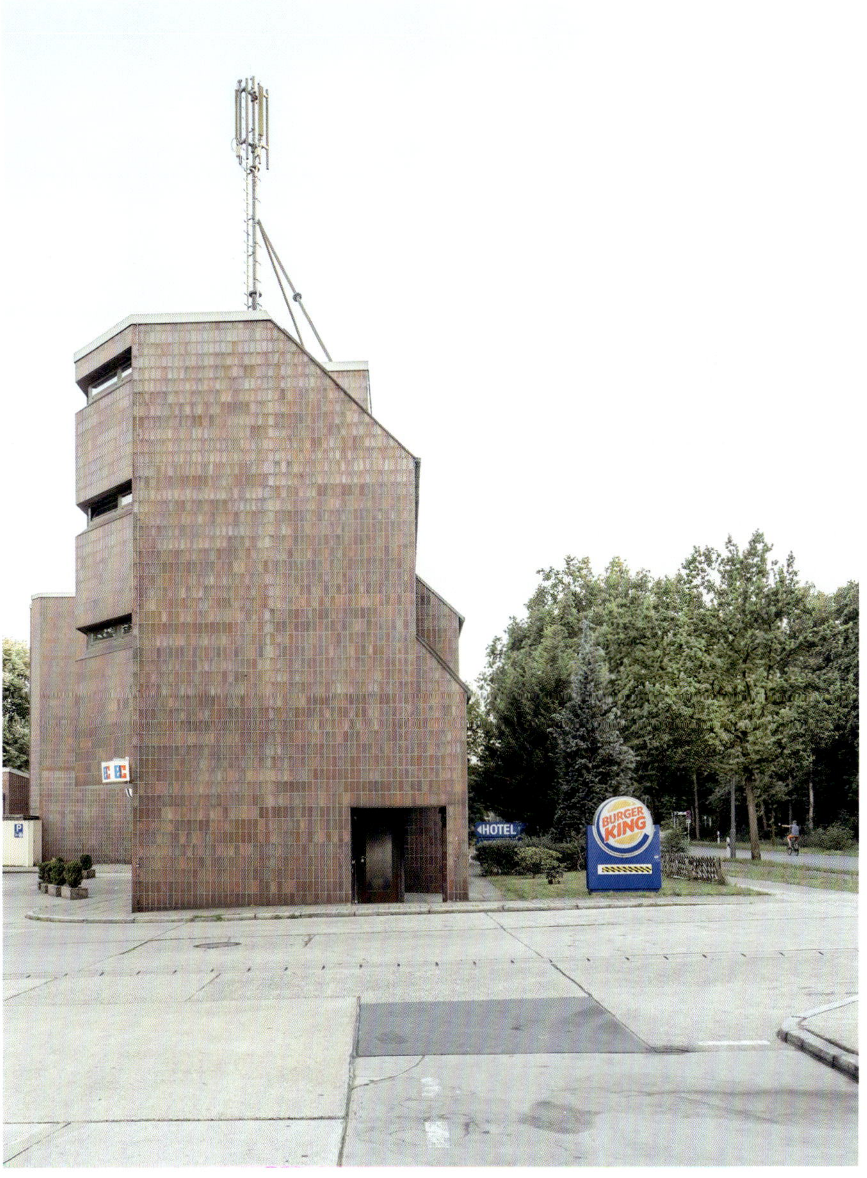
HOTEL
BURGER KING

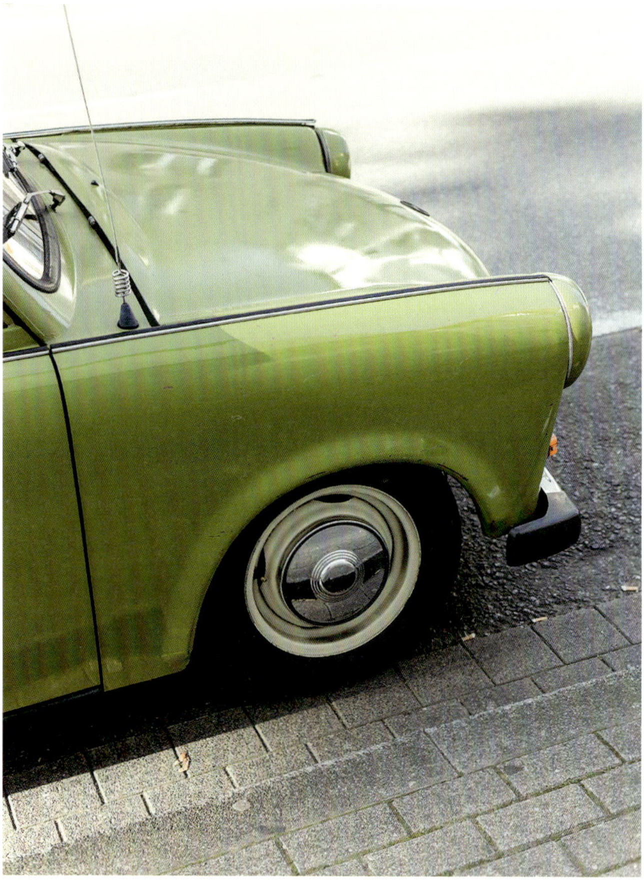

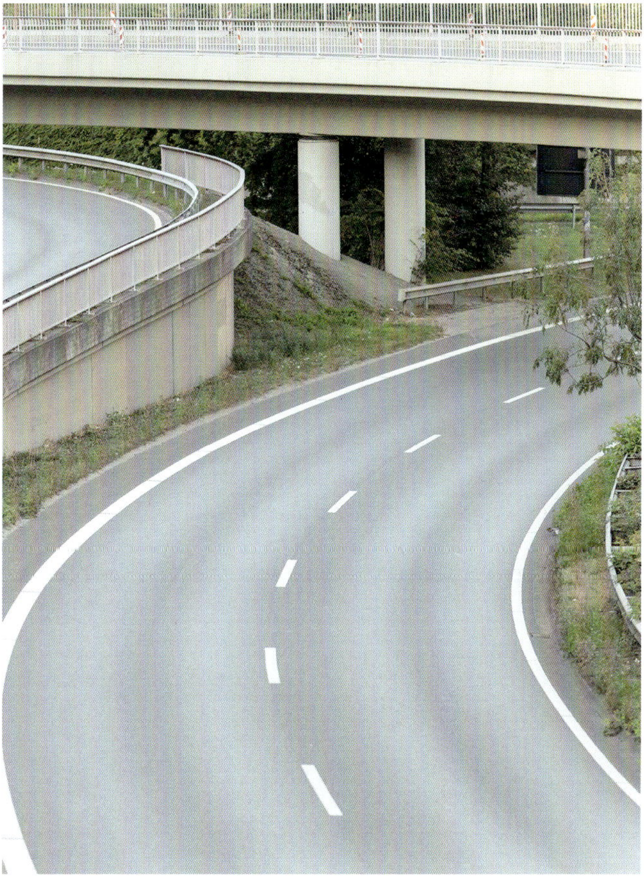

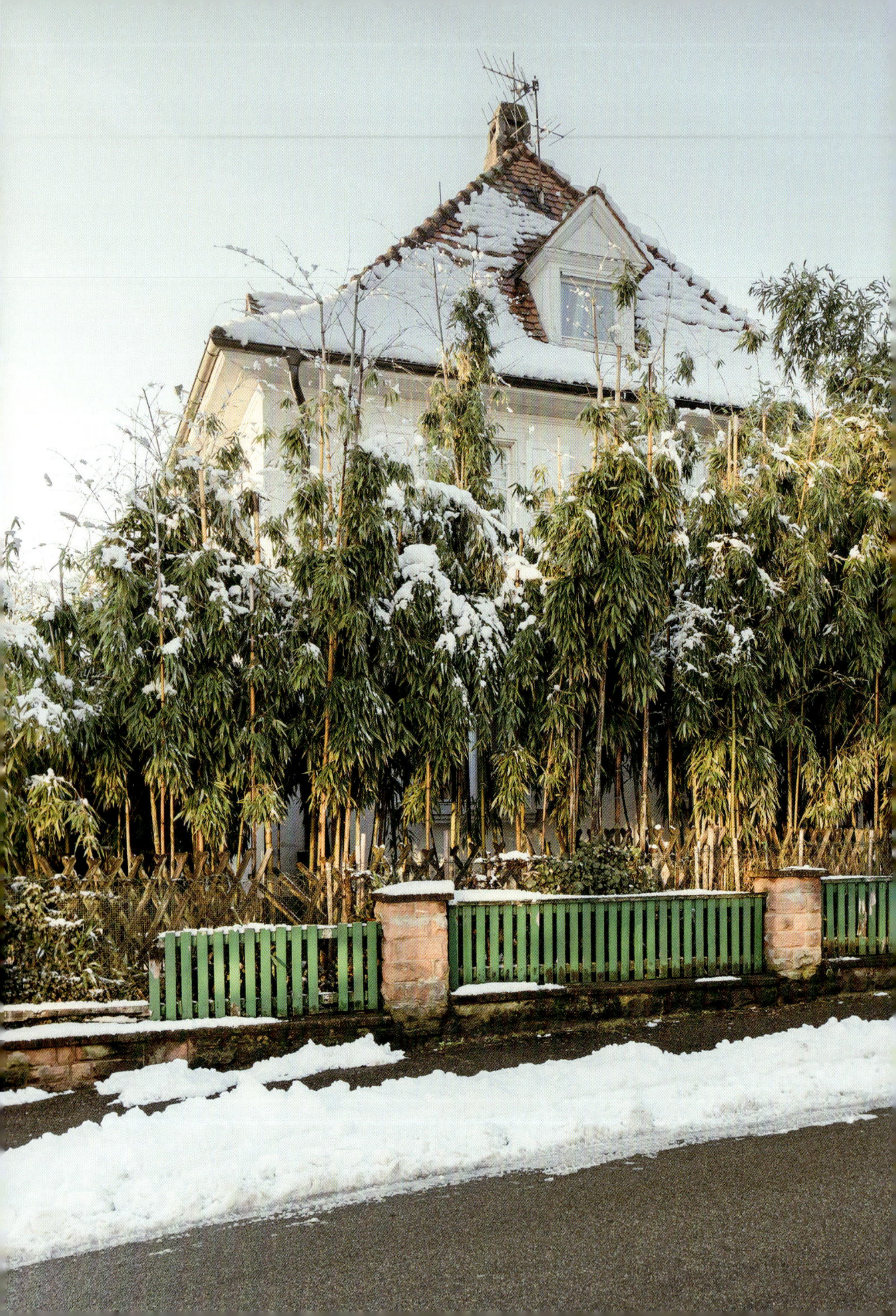

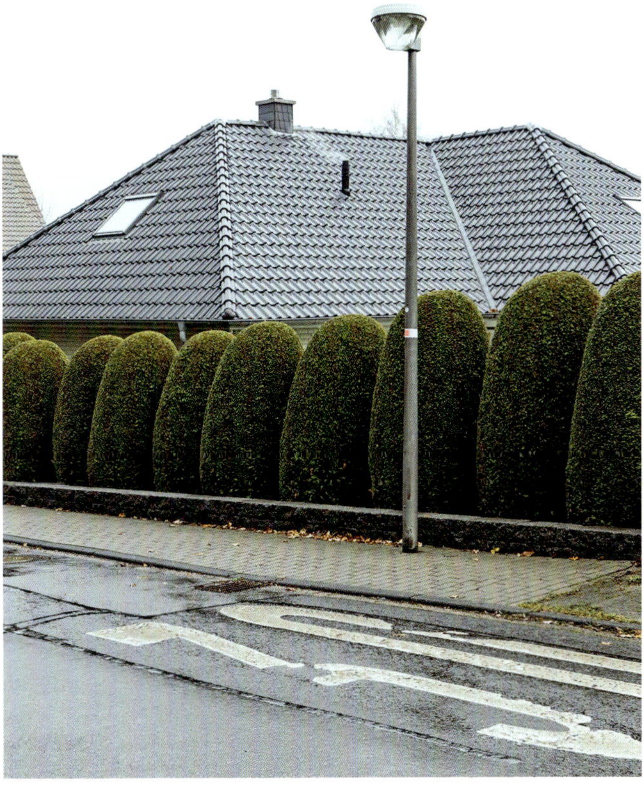

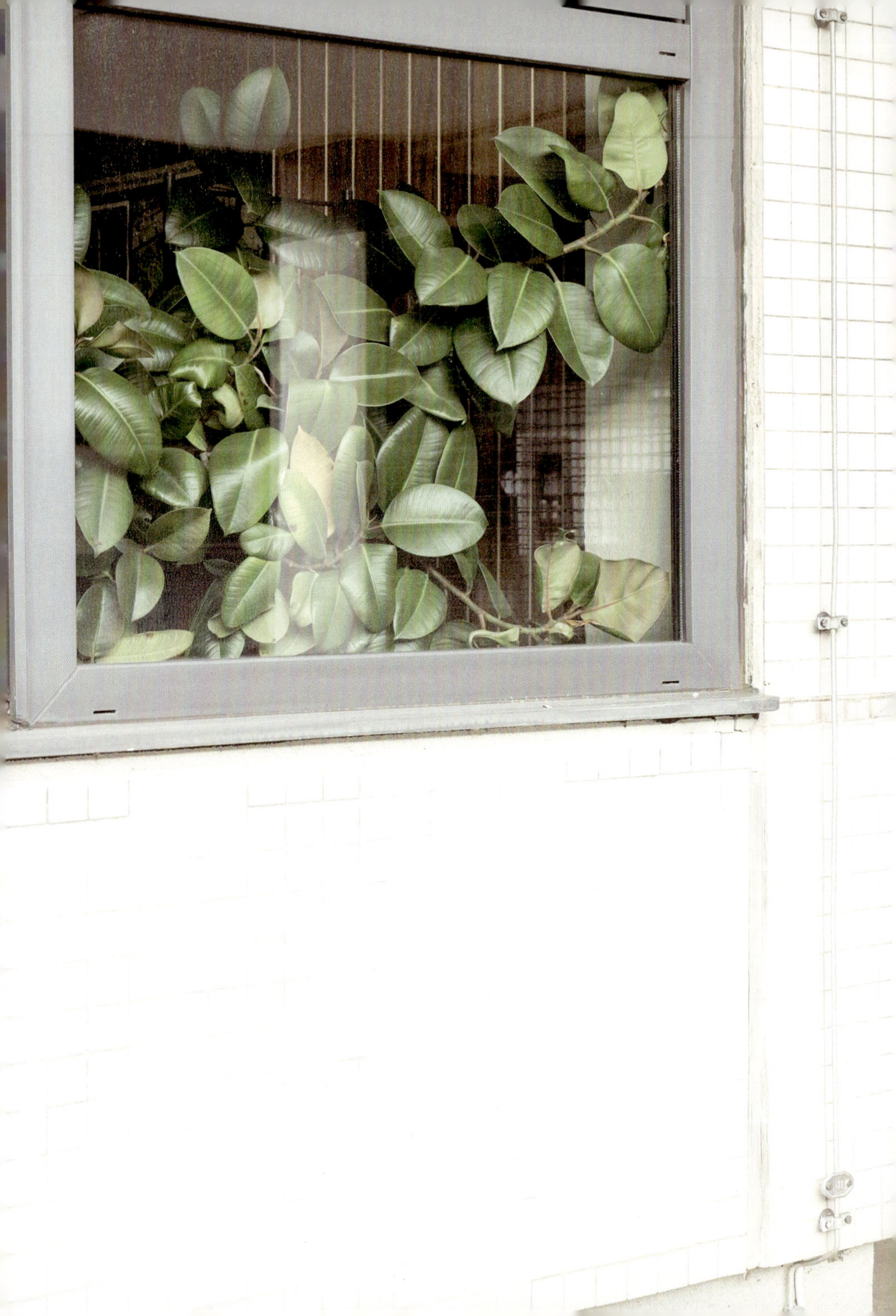

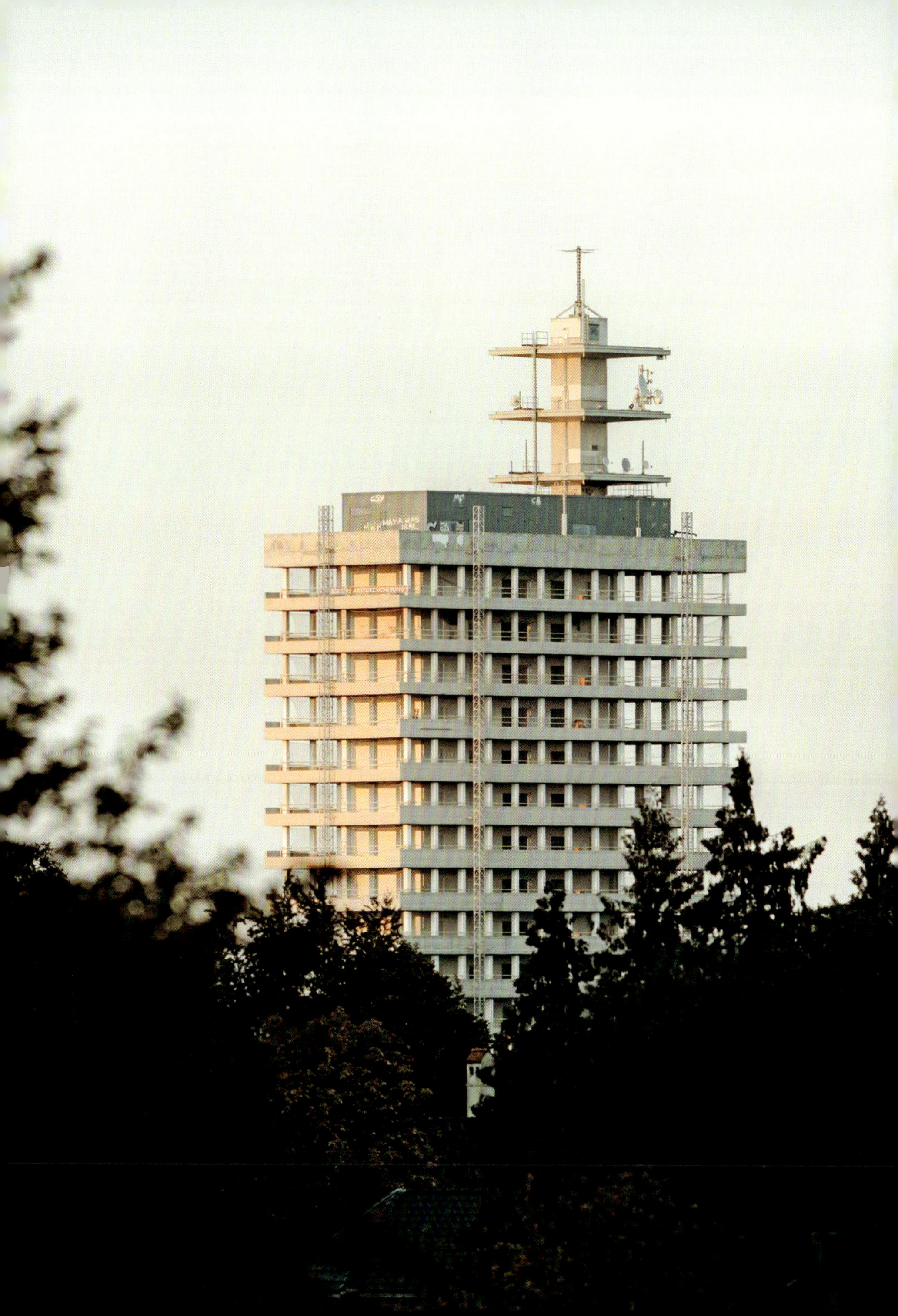

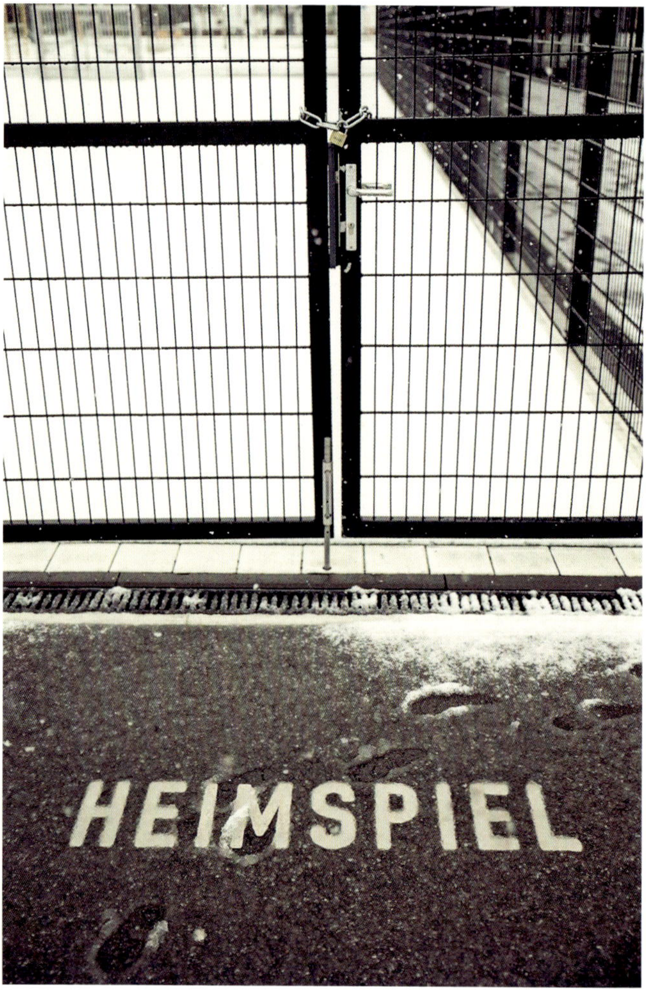
HEIMSPIEL

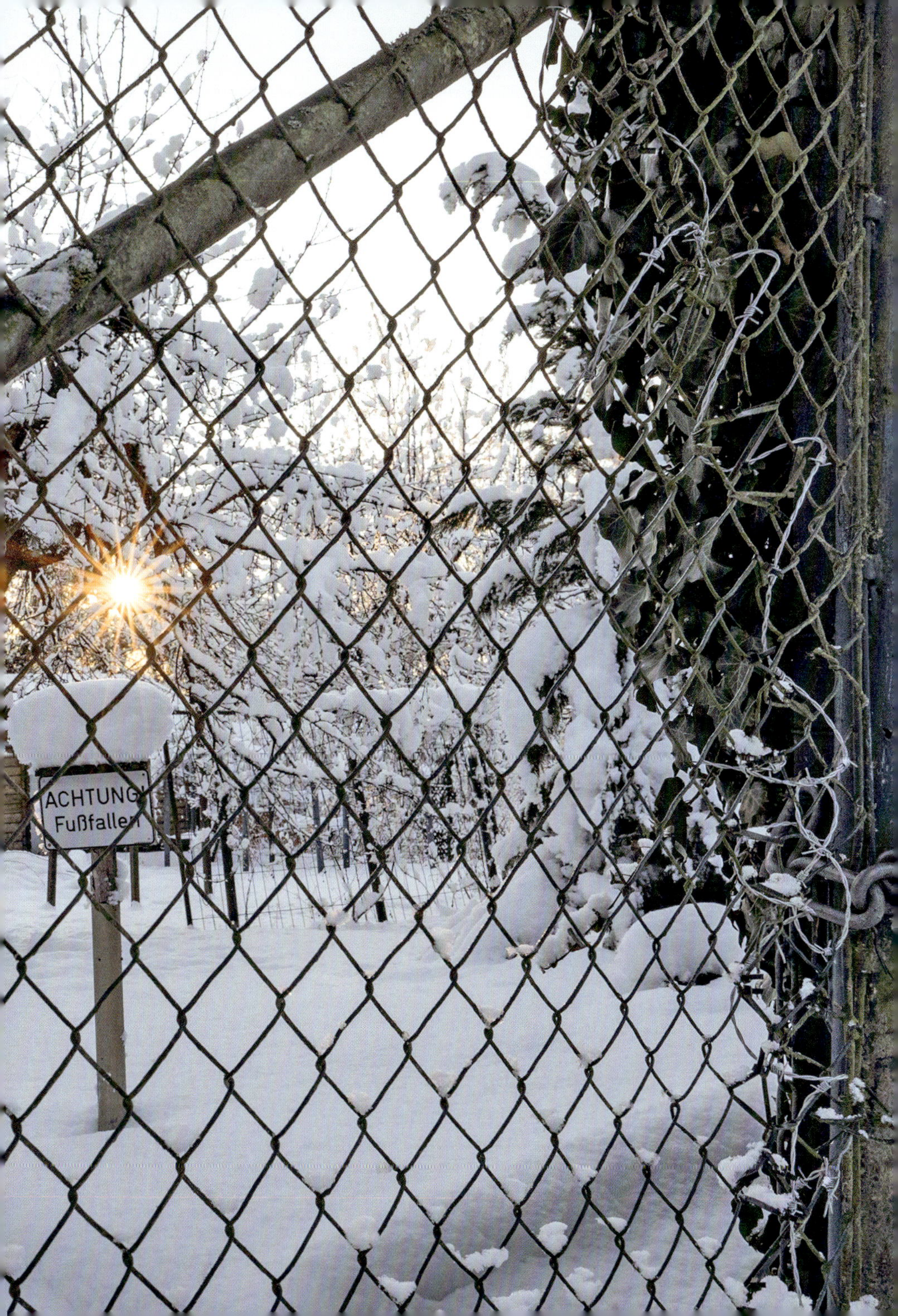
ACHTUNG
Fußfallen

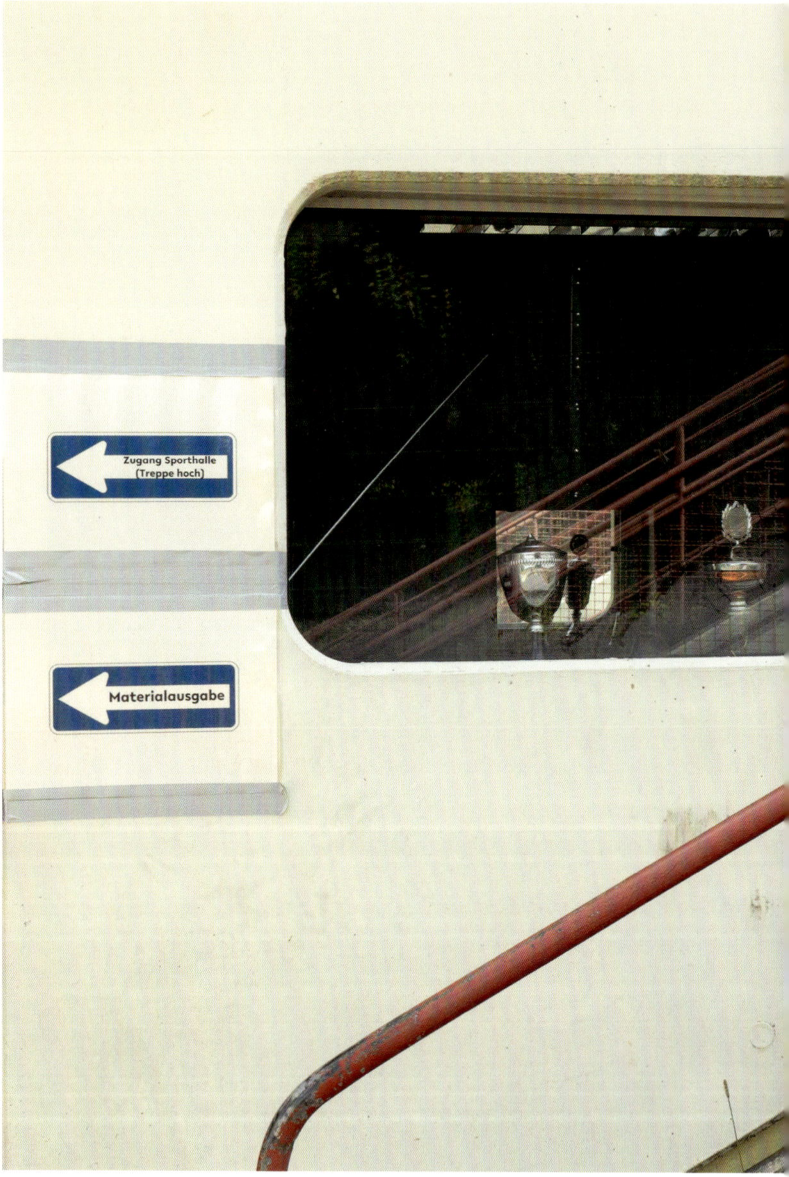
Zugang Sporthalle
(Treppe hoch)
Materialausgabe

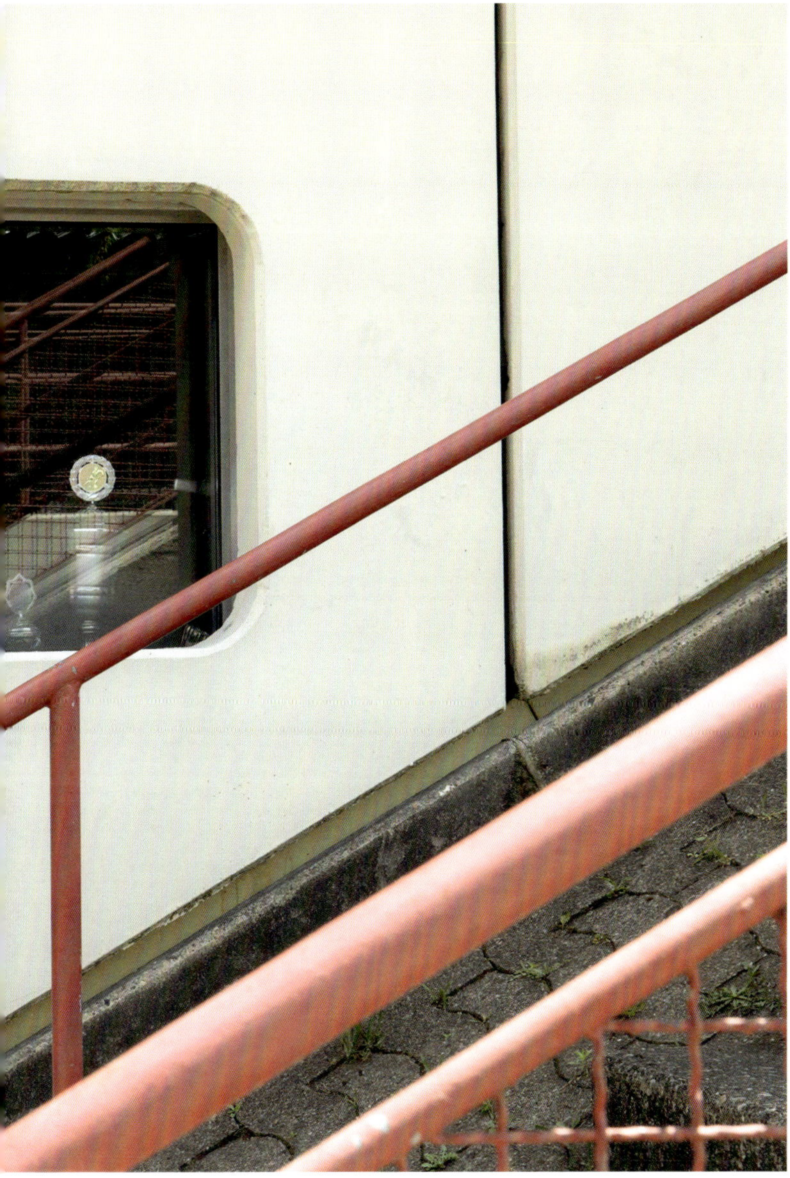

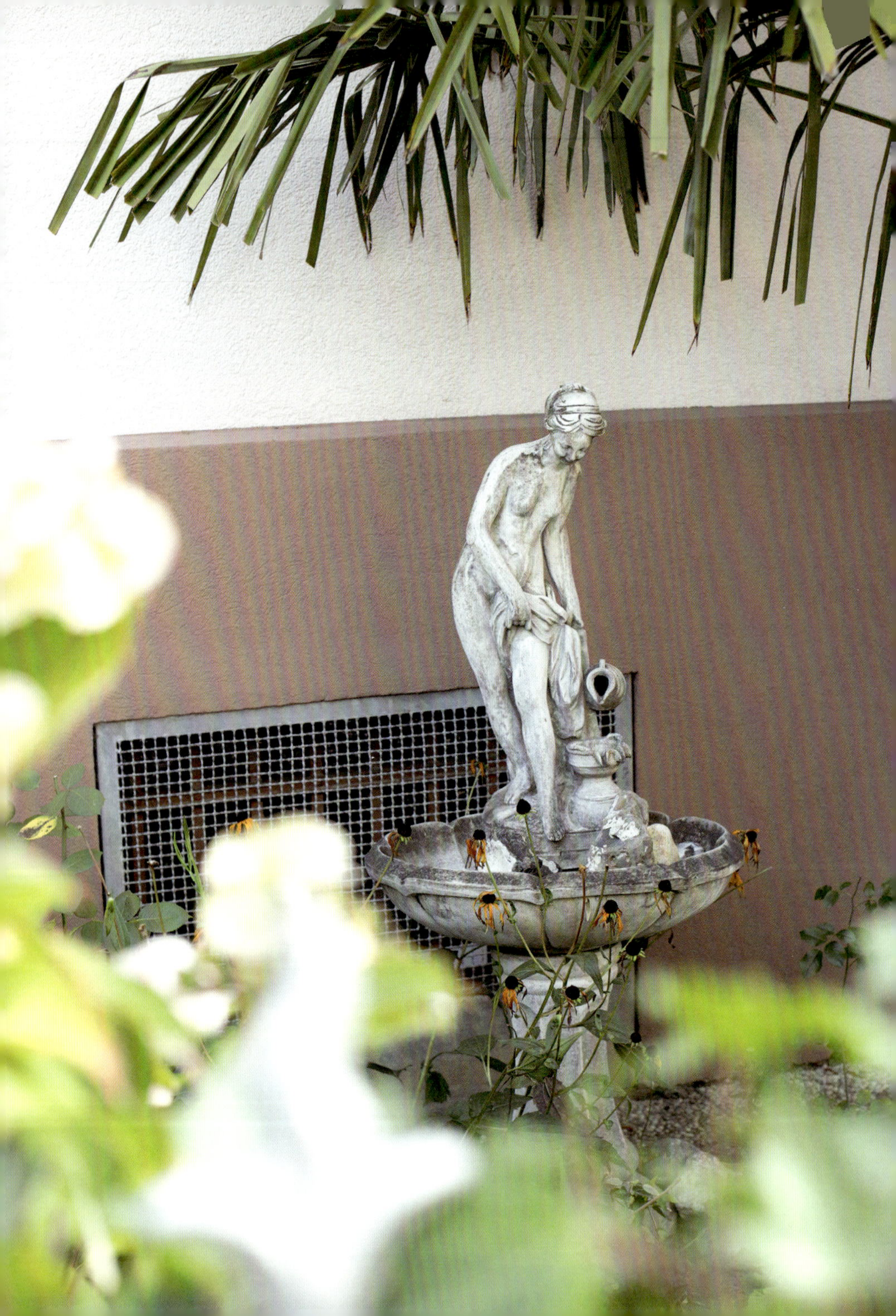

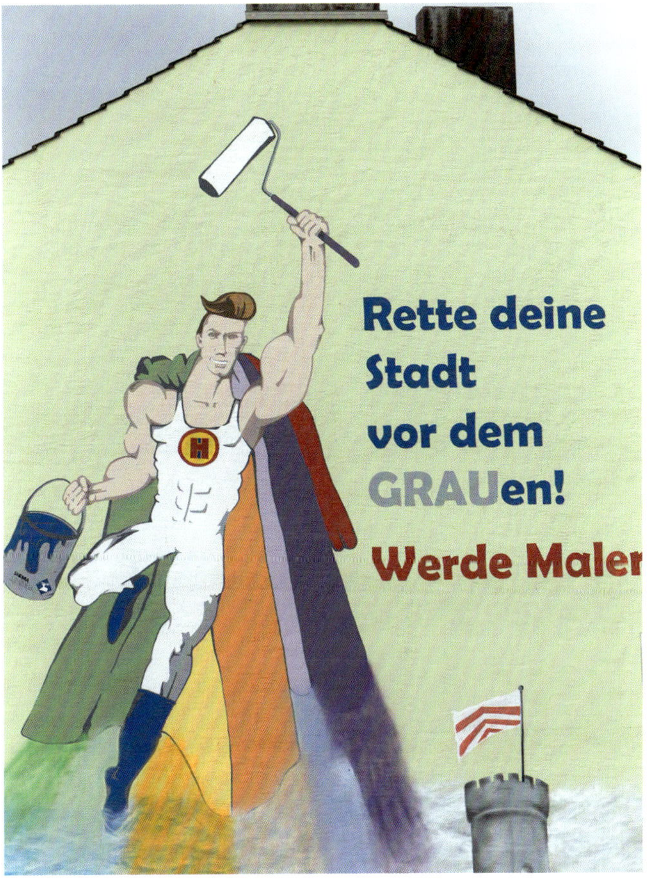
Rette deine
Stadt
vor dem
GRAUen!
Werde Maler

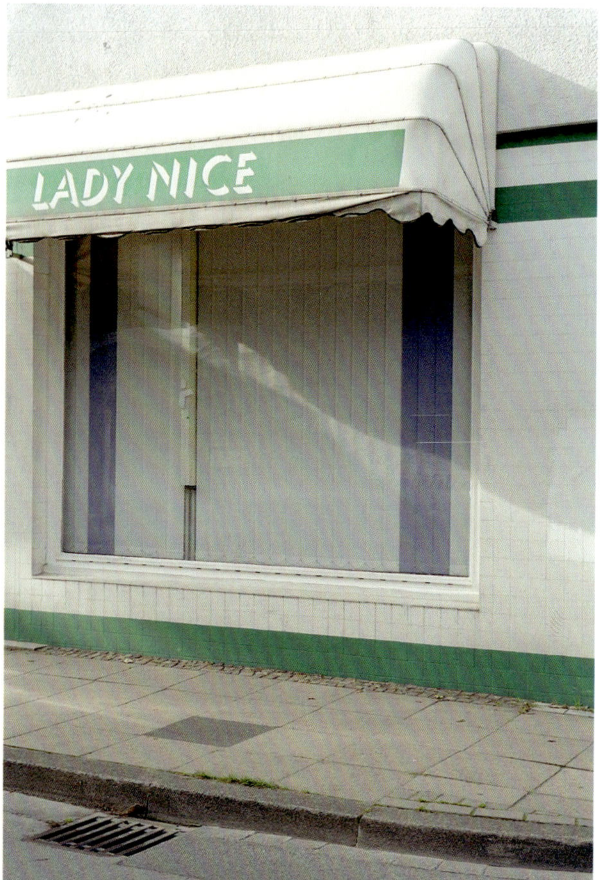
LADY NICE

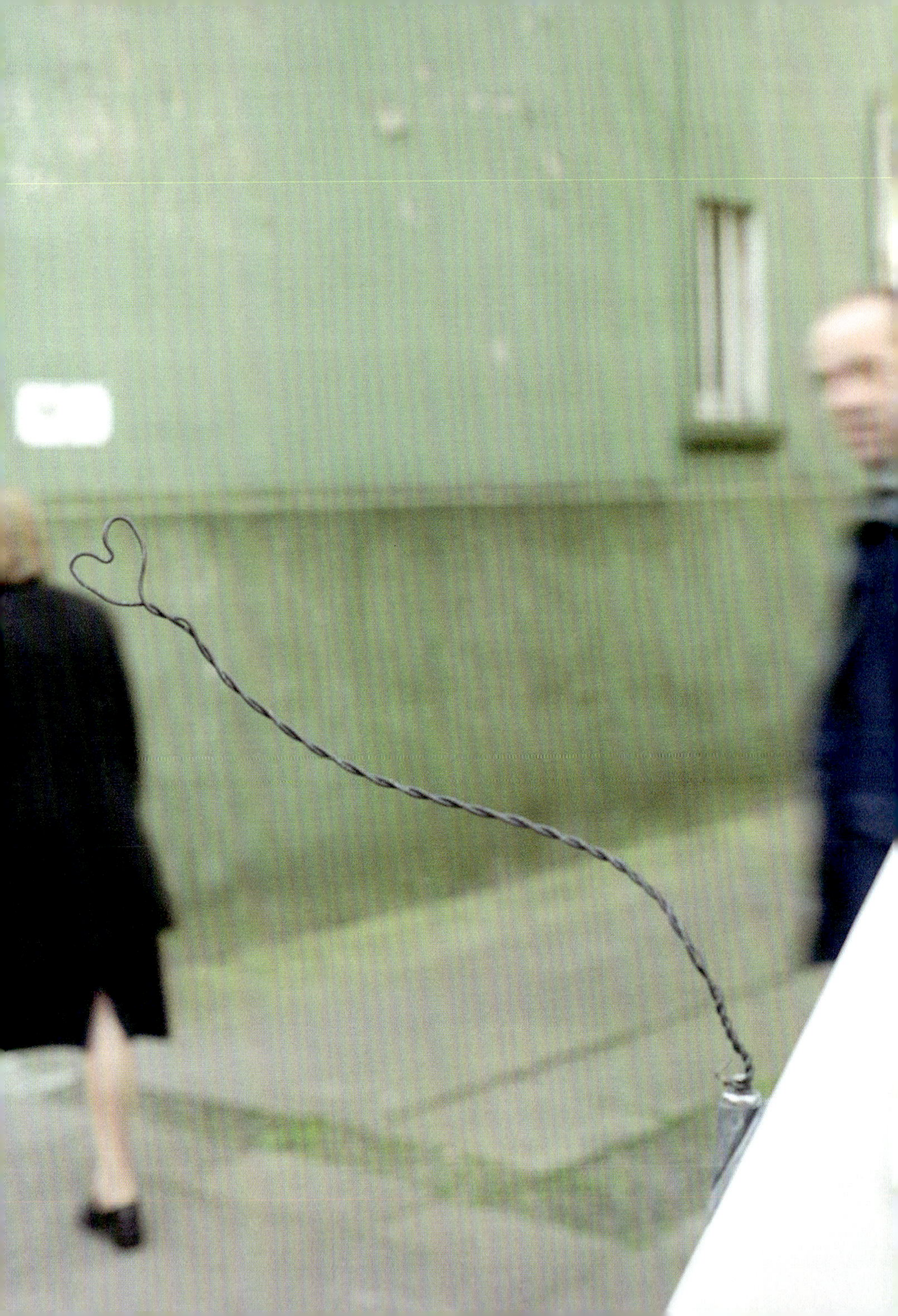

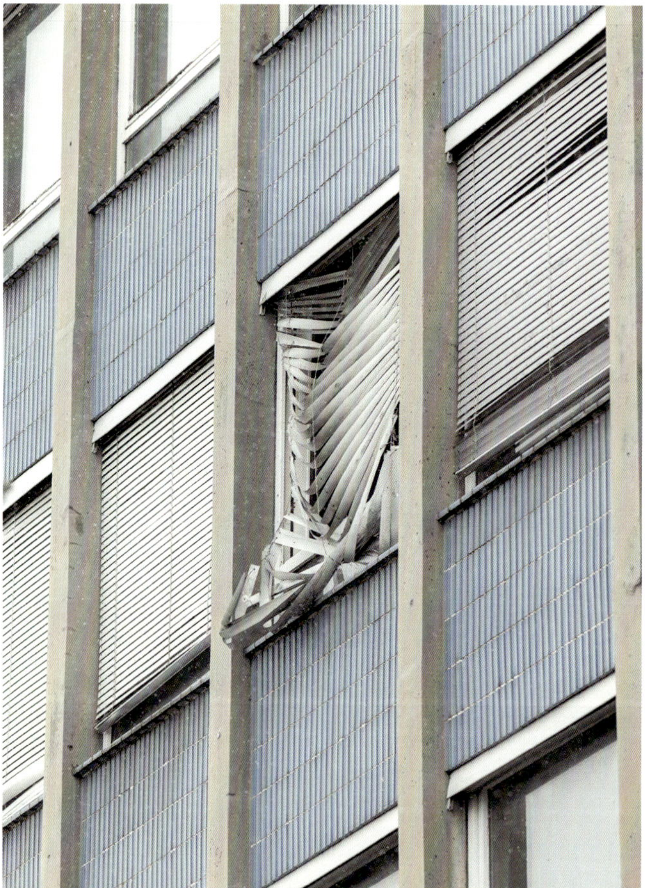

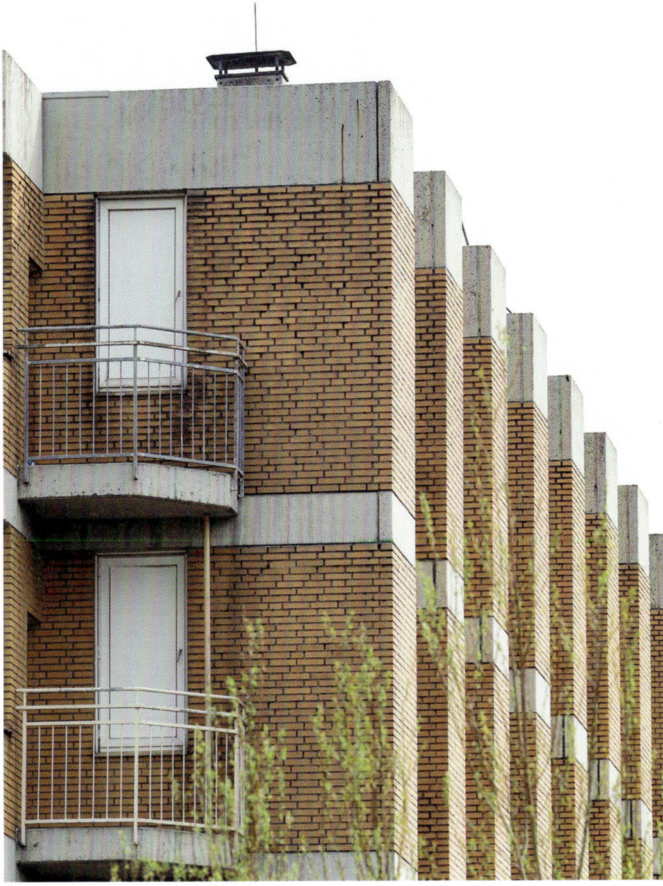

Iris Friedrichs Lebensräume

von Andreas Beaugrand

Jahrelang, lebenslang fahren die meisten Menschen von ihrem Zuhause zur Arbeit, zum Einkaufen, zum Treffen mit Freunden, in die Ferien und zurück – und auf einmal ist eine Häuserecke verschwunden, eine Straße neu geführt, ein neues Bauareal erschlossen. Es will nicht mehr gelingen, sich an das eben noch Gewohnte zu erinnern. Was war da? Wer lebte dort? Wie genau sah es aus? Man wird gewahr, dass sich das Leben zwischen reglosen und stummen Dingen einrichtet und die Gegenwart im Gewohnten verschwindet.

Die Bielefelder Fotografin Iris Friedrich widmet sich der Momentaufnahme gewöhnlichster Objekte. Das persönliche Umfeld und anonyme urbane Areale werden fotografisch neu präsent, in denen die Anwesenheit des Menschen selten ist, – und wenn, dann überrascht er; leicht sind Parallelen zu aktuellen gesellschaftlichen Situationen erkennbar.

Die Stille in den Fotografien, die Präsenz des Dargestellten und die Gunst des gewählten Augenblicks sind die Besonderheiten dieser Arbeiten, die an die Qualitäten des Stilllebens und die damit zum Ausdruck gebrachte Vergänglichkeit des Lebens erinnern. Ihnen wird gegenüber der Geschwindigkeit bewegter Bilder und der Produktion flüchtiger Gedanken in unserer schnelllebigen Zeit der Vorzug gegeben. Iris Friedrich hat ein spezifisches Interesse an den ambivalenten Erscheinungsweisen der Wirklichkeit und erzeugt daraus Fotografien, die ein kritisches, provokantes, ironisches und manchmal sogar poetisches Bild unserer Wirklichkeit entwerfen, um sich die Welt in Bildern wieder vertraut machen zu können, weil wir sie selbst nicht mehr wahrnehmen.

Der Philosoph Vilém Flusser hat diesen Umstand bereits 1983 verdeutlicht: „Die allgegenwärtigen technischen Bilder um uns herum sind daran, unsere ‚Wirklichkeit' magisch umzustrukturieren und in ein globales Bildszenarium umzukehren. Es geht hier im wesentlichen um ein ‚Vergessen'. Der Mensch vergißt, daß er es war, der die Bilder erzeugte, um sich an ihnen in der Welt zu orientieren. Er kann sie nicht mehr entziffern und lebt von nun ab in Funktion seiner eigenen Bilder: Imagination ist in Halluzination umgeschlagen. [...] Dieser scheinbar unsymbolische, objektive Charakter der technischen Bilder führt den Betrachter dazu, sie nicht als Bilder, sondern als Fenster anzusehen. Er traut ihnen wie seinen eigenen Augen. Und folglich kritisiert er sie auch nicht als Bilder, sondern als Weltanschauungen (sofern er sie überhaupt kritisiert)." [1]

Daran erinnert Iris Friedrich mit ihren Fotografien. Das Objektiv ihrer Kamera ist in keiner Weise objektiv, sondern durch den Moment, in dem sie den Auslöser betätigt, und die Auswahl der in diesem Buch gezeigten Arbeiten vermittelt sie den Betrachtern subjektive Blicke durch fotografische Fenster, durch Momentaufnahmen im wahrsten Wortsinne, die es uns ermöglichen, uns wieder bewusst in unseren alltäglichen Lebensräumen zu orientieren – und sie im selben Moment wieder zu verlassen: Als spannungsreichen Kontrast zu den zum Teil an Stillleben erinnernde Fotografien transferiert Iris Friedrich eine Reihe von ihnen in die virtuelle Realität. Mit dem Augmented Reality Tool Artivive können im Buch besonders markierte Fotografien eingescannt werden. Dann erscheinen auf dem Display ironisierende, karikierende, die auf den Fotos dargestellten Situationen überspitzende Bewegtbilder, die im wahrsten Wortsinne zu einer erweiterten Realität führen.

1. Vilém Flusser: Edition Flusser / hg. von Andreas Müller-Pohle, Bd. 3: Vilém Flusser: Für eine Philosophie der Fotografie, Göttingen 1997[8], S. 10. 14.

Iris Friedrich's Living Spaces

by Andreas Beaugrand

For years, often for a lifetime, most people spend hours driving from home to work, to go shopping, to meet friends, go on holiday and back. – Then suddenly a corner of a house disappeared, a street was rerouted, a new building developed. It is no longer possible to remember what was familiar a moment ago. What was there? Who lived there? What exactly did the space look like? Awareness arises that life settles in between regular and silent things and that the present disappears in the familiar.

Bielefeld photographer Iris Friedrich is dedicated to taking snapshots of the most everyday objects. Personal spaces and anonymous urban areas become alive photographically in a new way. The presence of people is rare and when they do appear, are often unexpected. Parallels to current social situations are easily recognizable.

The stillness in the photographs, the presence of the sitter and the favor of the chosen moment are the special features of these works. They recall the qualities of still life and the transience of life which they express. They are preferred to the speed of moving images and the production of fleeting thoughts in our fast-moving times. Iris Friedrich has a specific interest in the ambivalent manifestations of reality and uses them to produce photographs that create a critical, provocative, ironic and sometimes even poetic image of our reality. We can reacquaint ourselves with the world in pictures because we no longer perceive it ourselves.

The philosopher Vilém Flusser clarified this circumstance as early as 1983: „The technical images currently all around us are in the process of magically restructuring our 'reality' and turning it into a 'global image scenario'. Essentially this is a question of 'amnesia'. Human beings forget they created the images in order to orientate themselves in the world. Since they are no longer able to decode them, their lives become a function of their own images: Imagination has turned into hallucination. [...] This apparently non-symbolic, objective character of technical images leads whoever looks at them to see them not as images but as windows. Observers thus do not believe them as they do their own eyes. Consequently they do not criticize them as images, but as ways of looking at the world (to the extent that they criticize them at all)." [1]

Iris Friedrich reminds us of this with her photographs. The lens of her camera is in no way objective, but through the moment she presses the shutter release and the selection of works shown in this book, she provides viewers with subjective glimpses through photographic windows, snapshots in the truest sense of the word. These enable us to orient ourselves consciously in our everyday living spaces again – and to leave them again in the same moment: The augmented reality Artivive app allows the viewer to scan certain photographs marked with the Artivive icon by means of the smartphone. The viewer sees ironic, caricaturing moving images that exaggerate the situations depicted in the photos and literally lead to an augmented reality.

1. Vilém Flusser, Towards a Philosophy of Photography, London 2012. Originally published in German as *Für eine Philosophie der Fotografie*, Göttingen 1983.

AR animated

Begleitende Ausstellung | Accompanying exhibition:
GRAUMELIERT pepper and salt,
Kunstverein Oerlinghausen 16.01. – 27.02.2022

Herausgeberin | Editor:
Iris Friedrich
Instagram: iris_friedrich_photography

Fotografien und Bewegtbilder | Photographs and moving pictures:
Iris Friedrich

Cover:
Iris Friedrich | Courtesy of plainpicture GmbH

Texte | Texts:
Michael Ammann | Prof. Dr. Andreas Beaugrand

Gestaltung | Design:
stilwechseldesign | Pia K. Gätjen

Lektorat | Copyediting:
Gertrud Bach-Korth, Simone Schneider |
Susanne Fleig, Tamara Huggan

Übersetzung | Translation:
Prof. Dr. Andreas Beaugrand, Susanne Fleig, Tamara Huggan

Projektmanagement | Project Management, Kerber Verlag:
Lydia Fuchs

Herstellung | Production, Kerber Verlag:
Jens Bartneck

Gesamtherstellung | Printed and published by
Kerber Verlag
Windelsbleicher Str. 166–170
33659 Bielefeld | Germany
+49 521 950 08 10 | +49 521 950 08 88 (F)
info@kerberverlag.com | kerberverlag.com

Kerber Publikationen werden weltweit vertrieben: | Kerber publications are distributed worldwide:
ACC Art Books | Sandy Lane | Old Martlesham
Woodbridge, IP12 4SD | UK
+44 1394 38 99 50 | +44 1394 38 99 99 (F)
accartbooks.com | uksales@accartbooks.com

Artbook | D.A.P.
75 Broad Street, Suite 630 | New York,
NY 10004 | USA
+1 (212) 627-1999 | +1 (212) 627-9484 (F)
artbook.com | orders@dapinc.com

AVA Verlagsauslieferung AG
Centralweg 16 | 8910 Affoltern am Albis |
Switzerland
+41 44 762 42 50 | +41 44 762 42 10 (F)
avainfo@ava.ch

Zeitfracht GmbH
Verlagsauslieferung
kerber-verlag@zeitfracht.de

Die Deutsche Nationalbibliothek verzeichnet diese Publikation in der Deutschen Nationalbibliografie: dnb.de. | The Deutsche Nationalbibliothek lists this publication in the Deutsche Nationalbibliografie: dnb.de.

ISBN 978-3-7356-0833-8

www.kerberverlag.com
www.irisfriedrich.de
www.beaugrand-kulturkonzepte.de

Printed in Germany

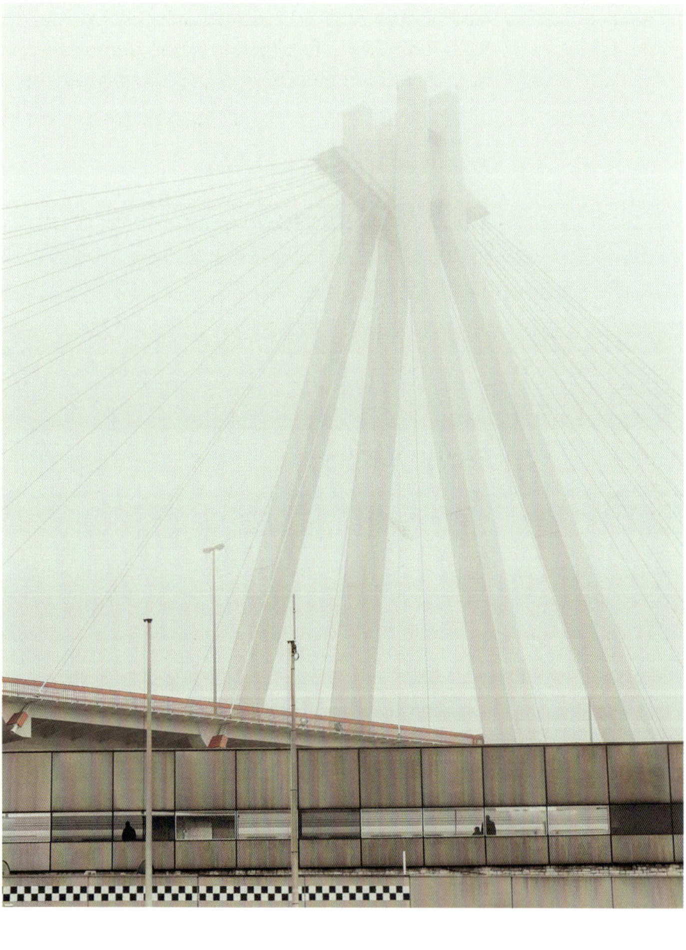

Dieses Projekt wurde partiell gefördert von der Stiftung Kulturwerk der VG Bild-Kunst und dem Ministerium für Kultur und Wissenschaft des Landes Nordrhein-Westfalen durch ein Künstlerstipendium im Rahmen der NRW-Corona-Hilfen.

This project was partially funded by the foundation Kulturwerk of VG Bild-Kunst and the Ministry of Culture and Science of the State of North Rhine-Westphalia (NRW) through an artist grant as part of the NRW-Covid-19 aids.

Bild Kunst
KULTURWERK

Ministry of Culture and Science
of the State of
North Rhine-Westphalia

Danke I Thank you

Mitwirkende | Starring

Rafael Leandro Hellweg | Dancer WAKE UP O.W.L. Young Company
Andreas Kaling | Bass Saxophone
Jonas Pfeiffer | Parkour
Tobi Schazmann | Gen Null and dancing UFOs: Milo Antic,
Leonie Heitz, Julia Henneberg, Sven Rosenkötter
Snowboarder | Skier: Jonas, Malou, Moritz, Niklas, Sergio
Zweiradteam: Luzie Schröder, Mia Schröder
Kinder im Laubhaufen | Kids in leaf pile: Mikkel, Paul

Musik | Music

Amarone string quartet Brandenburg an der Havel: Katrin Kösler,
Philippe Perotto, Violinen_Violins | Geraldo Brandigi, Viola | Joachim Köhler, Violoncello
Bellaire, AOC Records | Triple Double Production | Hadrien Azyme, FX Piat
Cut Spencer
Gen Null
Mardomi | Dominik Marchioni
Olivier | Olivier Kleine
Stecken & Ohrloch | Marko Hauburg, Stellan Krabbe, Nikolaus Woernle

Requisiteurin | Property Master

Marion Plaßmann | Bildhauerin | Sculptress

Unterstützung | Support

André Adomeit | Agentur für Arbeit Bielefeld_Employment Agency Bielefeld: Pressesprecher_Press spokesperson Matthias Hertle | Michael Ammann | Gertrud Bach-Korth | Barthouse: Nadine Barth | Gero Breloer | Elmar Brinkmöller | Imke Brunzema | Hermann Dreesbeimdieke | Drubba GmbH: Director Marketing Kathrin Maier | Filmhaus Bielefeld | Linus Fleig | Susanne Fleig | Ursula Fleig | Markus Friedemann | Agnes Friedrich | Heinrich Friedrich | Mikkel Friedrich | Pia Gätjen | Goldbeck GmbH: Architekt_Architect Siegfried Wendker und Teamleiterin Kommunikation and Team Lead Communications Dr. Judith Venjakob | Dieter Gutknecht | Veronika Heitz | Tamara Huggan | Tobias Jauch | KOELN-ART: Volker Hilgert | Kunstverein Oerlinghausen_Art Association Oerlinghausen: Andreas Beaugrand, Künstlerischer Leiter_Artistic Director | Schaustellerbetrieb Landwermann-Henschel GbR | Maarit Mittwoch | Dylan Mundt | Carsten Niemann | Simone Schneider | Stadtwerke Bielefeld GmbH_Municipal utilities Bielefeld GmbH: Unternehmenskommunikation_Corporate Communications Yvonne Liebold and Louis Schröter, Badleiter_Operations Manager Wiesenbad | Plainpicture GmbH, Roman Härer | Isadora Tast | Lenja Thees | Paul Thees and all the people who will support this project in the future.